One Hundred and One More Devotions

for Homeschool Moms

≫ ONE HUNDRED AND ONE ≪

More Devotions for Homeschool Moms

≫

Jackie Wellwood

CROSSWAY BOOKS

A DIVISION OF
GOOD NEWS PUBLISHERS
WHEATON, ILLINOIS

Cover design: Cindy Kiple

First printing, 2002

Printed in the United States of America

The Scripture passages are taken from the King James Version.

Library of Congress Cataloging-in-Publication Data
Wellwood, Jackie, 1959–
    101 more devotions for homeschool moms / Jackie Wellwood.
      p.   cm.
    ISBN 1-58134-383-3 (trade pbk. : alk. paper)
    1. Home school—Prayer-books and devotions—English. I. Title: One hundred and one more devotions for homeschool moms. II. Title: One hundred and one more devotions for homeschool moms. III. Title.
BV4847.W45   2002
242'.6431—dc21
                                          2001006921
                                            CIP

15	14	13	12	11	10	09	08	07	06	05	04	03	02
15	14	13	12	11	10	9	8	7	6	5	4	3	2	1

TABLE OF CONTENTS

Acknowledgments   9

Preface   11

1. Dreams   13

2. Clutterbug   15

3. I Give Up   17

4. Acceptance   19

5. Work Is Real Life   21

6. Perspective   23

7. Kindness   25

8. I Think I Can   27

9. I Heard What You Said, But What Did You Mean?   29

10. I Hate You   31

11. Be Careful   33

12. Weak Flesh   35

13. I Love You   37

14. I Had to Wait   39

15. Why Do I Need a Denim Jumper?   41

16. Too Many Tears   43

17. You Didn't Do . . .   45

18. Music Lessons   47

19. God Does the Testing   49

20. Pull Weeds Early   51

21. Please Don't   53

22. Respond Properly   55

23. God's Will   57

24. She Was Afraid   59

25. I Got Caught   61

26. Words Can Hurt   63

27. Redeem the Time   65

28. Talk Softly and Wait   67

29. He Sent Me Out   69

30. Are You Completely Dressed?   71

31. I Need to Talk   73

32. I Can Ski Again   75

33. He Blessed Me   77

34. I Can't Control People   79

35. Mom Is Glad at Me   81

36. What About My Schedule?   83

37. I'm Working on It   85

38. No Longer the Schoolmaster   87

39. Call on God   89

40. Hormonally Harassed   91

41. Go Back to Bed   93

42. I Am Running Away   95

43. God Is Good   97

44. It's Not Up to Me   99

45. God Sets the Priorities   101

46. A Good Example   103

47. She Didn't Do It   105

48. What Does He Think of Me?   107

49. Learning Is All the Time   109

50. She's at the End of Her Noodle   111

51. Discouraged by the Foolish   113

52. We Made It to the Parade   115

53. "Wasting Time"   117

54. Memorize It   119

55. Words Matter   121

56. Who Is in Control?   123

57. A Compassionate Wife   125

58. Learning the Letter Sounds   127

59. Perfect Peace   129

60. God Is the Power   131

61. Drip, Drip, Drip   133

62. Let's Get Organized   135

63. Lesson Plans   137

64. What Are You Thinking About?   139

65. What Did You Say?   141

66. Pass the Test   143

67. Ban Satan from School   145

68. Me, Homeschool?   147

69. Wait for the Fruit   149

70. A Bad Day   151

71. An Older Woman   153

72. A Sense of Humor   155

73. What's on the Calendar?   157

74. What Does Respect Look Like?   159

75. She Remembered Me   161

76. Spiritual Priorities   163

77. Do What You Can   165

78. Stop Crying   167

79. Obedience Has Benefits   169

80. The Electric Fence   171

81. The Flat Tire   173

82. Available to Help   175

83. Motivated by Failure   177

84. Focus   179

85. Following God's Will   181

86. Help Me, Lord   183

87. How Am I Motivated?   185

88. God Heals the Wounds   187

89. God Is the Leader   189

90. There Is Hope   191

91. Do They Feel Loved?   193

92. A Way to Help   195

93. Family Devotions   197

94. Don't Major on Minors   199

95. Not My Will   201

96. Treat Them Right   203

97. Family Influence   205

98. Communication 101   207

99. Fellowship with Families   209

100. The Flowers Died   211

101. No Control   213

Personal Reflections   216

ACKNOWLEDGMENTS

*I*t is getting more and more challenging to write books as a mom of many children. Without their cooperation and sacrifice I could not have completed this work. Their willingness to let me share their stories is a blessing. Without their gracious permission to tell you about their lives, I doubt I would have had much to say.

I have referred to my children in this book at different times in their lives. To make it simple, here are their ages at the time of the first printing of this devotional:

Jamie—seamstress—age fifteen

Jenny—meal coordinator—age thirteen

Jimmy—weather forecaster—age eleven

Jonathan—barn manager—age nine

Joanna—bookworm—age seven

Josiah—wants to be in charge—age five

Julianne—our "baby"—age three

Thank you to my husband, Jim, who did his best to lead his stressed-out wife through completion of this book during the first trimester of pregnancy. What a challenge!

Thank you to Mrs. "B" who encourages me when I need it the most.

Thank you to my editor, Ted Griffin, whose insight provided the needed improvements to the manuscript.

I could not put a book together without the help of my Lord, Jesus Christ. The past couple of years have been a time of intense spiritual challenge and growth. I am forever grateful for the Lord's help in showing me what needs to change and giving me the tools to do so. I am a work in process, and I am so glad that I don't have to figure it all out without Jesus.

PREFACE

I hope you enjoy depth in your daily devotions. As I reread these devotions, the thought struck me that there is a lot of meat here. I have tackled tough issues. I have talked about things that are not so pleasant. I have mentioned some things that most of us keep to ourselves. I have taken a chance on encouraging you in the process.

There are some dominant themes in this book such as being a good example to our children, relating properly to our husbands, trusting in the Lord for our provision, taming our tongue, and the value of training for character. These are the areas in my own life that the Lord is working on right now. I have not arrived yet, and in some cases it seems that forward movement is slow. Spiritual growth takes time. I need this book myself to remind me of what I need to be doing, particularly when the challenges come.

I have been transparent in this book in much the same way that I want to be honest with God. Hiding my failures does little to help me grow. On the other hand, sharing them with all of you is quite humbling. I believe that many of you are struggling with the same things that I have shared in this book. Seek the Lord for help, knowing that you are not alone in your struggles. My desire is that you will press on after gaining greater insight into yourself and God as you read through this devotional.

1

DREAMS

Commit thy way unto the LORD; trust also in him;
and he shall bring it to pass.

PSALM 37:5

⁓

*f*or five years I had wished for a place in the country. I expected that eventually we would move, even though my circumstances did not seem to indicate that a move to the country was possible. I struggled with this until one day I began to view this desire as a dream instead of an expectation. Each time I had expected that we would consider a move to the country I had been disappointed. Dreams don't disappoint. They are not expected to come true; so when they do it is exciting.

My husband and I had just decided to refinance our home to remodel our small kitchen so it would be more functional for our large family. Our three-bedroom, 1,250-square-foot home was fast becoming crowded. Although I was clueless about what else I could do to make our space work, I accepted that this house was God's best for me. I kept thinking that if God thought I needed a bigger house, then He would make it possible. *But He isn't doing that; so that must mean I need to be more creative with what I already have.* That was my thinking at the time.

Before we closed on our refinancing, my husband was informed that he was being promoted, possibly to a forty-hour-a-week position, which would not work as well with our family time as his twenty-four-hour shifts. He was going to turn down the promotion if it was not his regular twenty-four-hour shift. Family time was more important than a promotion. I was not happy since I saw not only my dream of living in the country disappearing, but also any hope of affording a larger home. I was a bit concerned. After sleeping on it one night I awoke the next day and proposed that we just drive to an area where we had considered living and see if we could afford to move there without the promotion. My husband agreed.

For the first time we were going out to the country and I did not have moving on my mind. We had already made our decision to stay in our suburban home a few more years. We randomly selected a real estate office and literally walked into our ten-acre farm with a house more than double the size of our old one. Outbuildings and fabulous neighbors made this better than my dream. God did it in His way in His timing. I wasn't trying to engineer the circumstances for a change. I still have a hard time believing that I am actually living my dream come true. Psalm 37:5 was printed on a card on the kitchen table as we walked through the house. I claimed that verse for our situation before we knew that we were buying the house. The farmer's wife had claimed it for the sale of their home too.

Do you have any dreams? Dream big dreams because if they are God's will for you they will come true.

PRAYER

Father, thank You, thank You, thank You. I hardly feel worthy of such a precious gift. ❧

FOOD FOR THOUGHT

1. Do your dreams seem unattainable?
2. How do your dreams line up with what you see as God's will for your life?
3. Memorize Psalm 37:5. Believe it!

2

CLUTTERBUG

*And he [Jesus] said unto them, Take heed, and beware of
covetousness: for a man's life consisteth not in the
abundance of the things which he possesseth.*

LUKE 12:15

❧

*I*n taking a look at Christian homes today, you would never know that the
verse above had any relevance to modern society. My home included. The tendency to want more and more feeds the problem of clutter. In many ways
my family's lifestyle of trying to get the minimum necessary to get the job done
has helped us. There are still areas, however, where the clutter seems to
abound.

I love books—books for me and books for the children. I like to sew.
Fabric on sale is a great help to the budget. I enjoy garage sales. There's
nothing quite like finding decorative wooden shelves for a couple of dollars.
My husband likes tools. Each one is going to be used in training our sons.
My children use a lot of crayons. *Too many*, I thought as my three-year-old
Joanna was tapping a crayon on her dinner plate. I wondered where that came
from since I thought we had put them all away.

Too much stuff distracts us from our tasks. If a workspace is cluttered
with stuff, it is difficult to be productive or even to use it at all. I have a desk
that is useless most of the time because it tends to attract piles of "important" papers. Much of what we have is truly useful and desirable for us to have

in our home. But there needs to be criteria to determine where these items belong and how many of them to have in the first place. It is wise to limit how much will come into your home.

Small homes are a blessing if you allow this finite space to define how much you have. If you do not continue to cram stuff into every available space (I have done this), then you will have your focus more appropriately on what God values as important—the training of your children. Too much stuff requires too much cleaning, rearranging, and overall maintenance. Much of it is unnecessary anyway.

Are you buying into the world's philosophy that more is better? In what subtle ways does this way of thinking complicate your life?

PRAYER

Lord, help me to see just how much I really need, and let me look for no more than that. Teach me to use less and to enjoy it more. Show me where I can simplify my school materials and get rid of what is not needed. Remind me that it is not how much I have, but what I do with what I have that pleases You most.

FOOD FOR THOUGHT

1. What is the minimum amount of materials (curriculum, paper, pencils, etc.) you need for your homeschool? How much more do you have than this?
2. Do you have some items that should be given away or sold? Do it! Apply the same principle to all areas of your home. Rejoice as you declutter and simplify.
3. Jesus was an incredible teacher, but He taught without all of the stuff we use. How did He do it? What can we learn from Jesus that would lighten our load (clutter)?

3

I GIVE UP

Be of good courage, and he shall strengthen your heart,
all ye that hope in the LORD.

PSALM 31:24

❧

I like to work hard. I enjoy giving my best effort to whatever I am working on. One day in the early spring I think I overdid it. It was March, and we had baby goats that needed to be bottle-fed. It was our first year on the farm, and we had lost a few of the kids (that's farm talk for baby goats) during their births. We were adjusting to this reality and taking care of the remaining kids as best we knew how.

I had been up past midnight four nights in a row. Getting up at 7:00 A.M. each day allowed me no reserves to fall back on. I was exhausted. My husband was working overtime, and all of the responsibilities in our home fell on my shoulders. It was too much. I had no courage. I was vacillating between yelling and crying and finally sent myself into time-out. In the afternoon I took a bath, crawled into bed, and eventually got up and did a little more schoolwork with my seven-year-old.

Providentially my friend called me that day. She is the one who really understands me, and God used her to strengthen my heart. Sometimes the demands are just too much, and I make the mistake of not only trying to reach my potential but of exceeding it. That works very poorly. There are days when you won't be able to handle it all. Only do what is most important, and let go of the rest. Take care of yourself! Extended periods of sleep deprivation coupled with a staggering workload make a homeschool mother unable to be very effective in her roles.

Don't forget that your hope is in the Lord. It is not in your circumstances, your husband, your abilities, or anything else. Courage to persevere does not come from doing our work in our own power. Our flesh is not strong enough. God's strength is what keeps us daily serving Him in the tasks we are called to do. Courage to press on comes from knowing as we hope in Him that it is God who strengthens our heart. That's a promise.

Are you ready to give up? Don't do it. Seek your hope in the Lord, and He will strengthen you.

PRAYER

Dear Lord, I confess my tendency to work in my own power. I forget how much more I can do when I seek You to strengthen me and give me courage. You would not have called me to do something I could not do with Your help. Forgive me for forgetting this so often. Thank You for giving me hope that I can do it when I seek You first. ❧

FOOD FOR THOUGHT

1. Evaluate your workload. Are you trying to do too much?
2. Prayerfully seek God as you seek to understand yourself. Do you rely on God to strengthen you, or do you work hard using your own abilities to the point of exhaustion?
3. Take time each day to pray for guidance and direction regarding priorities. Watch for signs in your life that you have more courage as you see God strengthen your heart.

4

ACCEPTANCE

And they brought young children to him [Jesus], that he should
touch them: and his disciples rebuked those that brought them.
But when Jesus saw it, he was much displeased, and said unto them,
Suffer the little children to come unto me, and forbid them not:
for of such is the kingdom of God.

MARK 10:13-14

Joanna at five years old would often ask me to play or read a story to her. Invariably she picked a busy time to make her requests. I realized that when I would turn her away and say, "We'll do it later," later never came or I forgot. This probably does not surprise you, because we all do this from time to time. The problem is that we communicate rejection when we don't stop and make time for our children.

I don't like to be interrupted constantly. Homeschooling a large family has allowed me to become more flexible in this area. Just as I began to write this devotion, my four-year-old Josiah stopped by my office to ask a question. Only a couple of sentences later, Joanna had a problem that I needed to help her solve. It took talking to her ten-year-old brother Jimmy to straighten out the situation. Interruptions are part of homeschooling.

There are times to require the children to wait, but this should not be all of the time. I am glad that my children like to talk to me. They need to have access to me. They should be able to get near me. Sometimes the cares and commitments of life threaten to overtake our special time with our children. Bills do need to be paid, housework and meals take time, and a host of other things require our attention. Jesus was a busy man. How did He handle the interruptions?

Jesus was not too busy for the children. He welcomed them when the disciples thought He had more important matters to attend to. Jesus is our example. What He valued is what we should value. We have made being with our children easier on ourselves by homeschooling them. But it is possible to be with your children and not pay attention to them. Joanna does not complain when I turn her away when I am busy, but she certainly does not feel acceptance from me at such a time either. Ironically she shows her acceptance of me with her beautiful smile.

Do your children feel accepted by you? If not, how will they know how much Jesus loves and accepts them?

PRAYER

Heavenly Father, I thank You for sending Jesus to model love for me. The way He responded to the children who wanted to see Him shows me how to respond to my own children. I need Your help in this area because I am not very good at juggling all of my responsibilities. Please help me to work better with many interruptions so I can give my children the attention to their needs that communicates love and acceptance to them. ❧

FOOD FOR THOUGHT

1. What makes you feel rejected? Does this give you some ideas on how to communicate acceptance to your children?
2. Reflect on the powerful work of Jesus and the way He allowed the children to "interrupt" Him. Let God show you where you can change to be more like Jesus.
3. Be sensitive to your children and their needs.

5

WORK IS REAL LIFE

In the sweat of thy face shalt thou eat bread,
till thou return unto the ground; for out of it wast thou taken:
for dust thou art, and unto dust shalt thou return.

GENESIS 3:19

❧

At breakfast one Saturday morning I told the children why I require them to work hard at jobs they don't like as well as the ones they do. "Right-hand" jobs are things they like or are especially gifted at doing. "Left-hand" jobs are the unpleasant tasks or the difficult ones that someone has to do. A left-hand job might be changing the baby's diaper. A right-hand job might be mowing the yard with the tractor. All of life is made up of a combination of right- and left-hand jobs.

I showed the children that I have two hands, a right one and a left one. Both of our hands work together to get things done. I held up my hands clasped together. They balance each other out. One hand is usually stronger than the other. We favor the stronger hand. But we learn to use the other hand too. Some people are ambidextrous, meaning they can use both of their hands equally well. This enables many of them to be unusually skillful.

I want my children to grow up able to take right- and left-handed jobs in stride since this is real life. While their skill level in the right-hand jobs might be better, they can be competent in the left-hand jobs too. Even more important is the attitude they have toward the left-hand jobs. We all have to work. We all have to do some jobs we would rather not do. Our happiness is not found in eliminating all of the left-hand jobs, but in learning to have a good attitude toward them.

The children need to learn this while they are young so they can thrive whether they are doing something they like or are having to deal with the unpleasant issues of life. In our home it is easier for me to assign work based on preferences. I have enough children to do this fairly well. But how will my children learn to embrace the left-hand jobs in their life if I tend to give them only right-hand jobs? It is better to assign everyone some tasks they find unpleasant and help them learn to accept them with a right attitude.

How is your attitude right now? Are there days where homeschooling feels like a left-hand job for you?

PRAYER

Dear Lord, I thank You for showing me such a simple way to illustrate the jobs we like and those we don't for my children. Please show me how to help them develop good attitudes toward the more unpleasant tasks in life. Help me to be bold in requiring them to do the jobs nobody wants to do with an eye toward their future success. I pray for wisdom to know how to encourage them while they are struggling to learn these truths. ❧

FOOD FOR THOUGHT

1. Make a list of jobs around your home that are appropriate for the ages of your children. Circle the less desirable or harder jobs, and make sure each child gets at least one.
2. Memorize Genesis 3:19 as a family.
3. Praise right attitudes toward work more than performance.

6

PERSPECTIVE

And as it is appointed unto men once to die,
but after this the judgment.

HEBREWS 9:27

❧

After a "normal" morning of homeschooling I headed outside for a brisk half hour of cross-country skiing. My "normal" morning consisted of a two-year-old who needed constant direction, a four-year-old who needed an activity that both engaged him and kept him calm, book work with the six- and eight-year-olds, supervision of the nine-year-old, and study time for the twelve- and fourteen-year-olds. The morning went well, but I already felt spent for the day.

As I started across our field I noticed a number of cars traveling up our quiet road. They were going to the cemetery a half mile from our home. A woman in her early thirties had died of pneumonia, leaving a husband and two young children behind. Many thoughts flooded my mind as I realized this woman no longer could homeschool if she wanted to.

I take for granted that this all-consuming lifestyle will go on forever, but truly it will not. Our children will grow up and leave to have lives of their own. It could end sooner through unexpected death. As tedious as the days are, there are no guarantees that we will get even one more day to homeschool. We've heard the phrase "live every day as if it were your last." If you translate this into "take each day of homeschooling and do your best because you may not get another day," it is motivating.

The only time that we know we have is the present. Yesterday is gone, and tomorrow may not come. Taking days individually is refreshing. Then the work doesn't seem so overwhelming. One day at a time can be pretty manageable. Each day begins afresh, and we can make it whatever we want. Homeschooling offers great freedom to us as we explore different ways to teach and learn. Just remember to embrace each day as though you may not have another one to homeschool.

It was sobering for me to see the cars lining up to go to the cemetery for the burial of the young woman. The finality of death gave me a chill as I skied back to the house. My morning had been quite a challenge, just as the afternoon promised to be. But at least I was still here with my children. I still had the opportunity to train them at home. I still had the rest of the day to encourage them.

How long do you have left to homeschool? Could it be shorter than you think?

PRAYER

Dear Jesus, thank You for each and every day that You give me to homeschool my children. Forgive me for taking for granted that I will always be able to do this. There are no guarantees for the future. Help me to make better use of the present in my service to You. ❧

FOOD FOR THOUGHT

1. What is your perspective? Do you put off until tomorrow what you should be doing today? Rethink your plans in terms of Hebrews 9:27.
2. If your time in eternity happens sooner than you expect, do you have any plans for someone to continue homeschooling your children after you are gone?
3. Thank God for each precious day you have with your children.

7

KINDNESS

Charity suffereth long, and is kind; charity envieth not;
charity vaunteth not itself, is not puffed up.

1 CORINTHIANS 13:4

❧

Jimmy (age nine) and Jonathan (age seven) are thoughtful boys. One day I saw the flag up on our mailbox. I did not think we had mail in there that needed to be picked up, so I asked the boys about it. They told me they had put rubber bands there for our mail carrier to pick up to reuse to bundle our mail. This act of kindness seems almost too insignificant to be noticed. This is from our perspective though.

Even the smallest acts of kindness can mean so much to other people. Making a favorite meal for your husband or taking your children to the park may not seem like much to you, but these acts of kindness are outward manifestations of your love. How good it is for our children to learn early in life to take initiative in little acts of kindness for other people. Brothers and sisters can learn much about caring for a wife or a husband as they learn how to be kind to each other.

Homeschooling offers us extraordinary opportunities to train boys and girls how to treat each other properly. The widely accepted cultural norm that it is okay for boys and girls to tease each other has no place in our homes. Children who grow up teasing each other turn into spouses who do the same. It is far better for us to initiate thinking about acts of kindness toward brothers and sisters.

Recently our four-year-old Josiah has been particularly sensitive to the needs of his three-year-old sister Julianne. While these ages tend to compete with each other and need much help learning to get along, I have seen a tender side in Josiah that I want to nurture. It is common for him to want to pour her cereal and her milk for her. When Josiah exhibits an act of kindness like this toward Julianne, I praise him for being kind. And Julianne likes it when Josiah takes care of her. As I reinforce acts of kindness in our family, I am teaching our children how to show love. Wrong actions and attitudes toward each other can be turned around with acts of kindness.

Are your children kind to each other? Have you given them a good example of kindness?

PRAYER

Dear Jesus, what a model of love You are for me. Your acts of kindness are examples to our family. Please help me to facilitate relationships between the boys and girls in our family that honor You by their kindness. I pray that a desire to be kind to others would become a part of each one of the lives of our children.

FOOD FOR THOUGHT

1. Make a list together with your children of different acts of kindness. Post this list as a reminder as you develop this way of thinking in them.
2. Look for acts of kindness to perform outside of your home such as visiting older people or taking meals to the needy.
3. Offer your husband a drink when he comes home, give him a back rub, wash his car, etc. in front of your children, so they understand that kindness is good in a marriage.

8

I THINK I CAN

And Moses said unto the LORD, O my Lord, I am not eloquent,
neither heretofore, nor since thou hast spoken unto thy servant:
but I am slow of speech, and of a slow tongue. And the LORD said
unto him, Who hath made man's mouth? or who maketh the dumb,
or deaf, or the seeing, or the blind? Have not I, the LORD?
Now therefore go, and I will be with thy mouth, and
teach thee what thou shalt say.

EXODUS 4:10-12

All of us have limitations that we think limit our service for the Lord. We may feel we don't have the drive or the energy to follow God's call. I wrestled with God's call to speak and write for about four years. Although I saw my first two books published during this time and had a number of speaking engagements, I was dragging my feet because I didn't think I could be the proper wife and mother if I spread myself so thin. I didn't understand that when God calls you, He is right there to overcome the obstacles.

Homeschooling is a high calling. It requires so much of us that it would be easy to decide we are not up to the task. I have heard women say that it is okay for me to homeschool, but they just can't do it. I can't do it either! I feel like Moses. He didn't think he had what it took to lead the Israelites. It was a big and challenging job. God's response to the concerns of Moses is applicable to our reservations about homeschooling.

God told Moses He would tell him what to say. Moses was afraid that his weak area, communication, would prevent him from answering God's call. God provided what Moses needed to get the job done, just as He will for us when we ask Him. Disorganization, anger, and illness are just some of the weaknesses that might handicap us. In each of our weak areas we must cry out to God, so that He hears our request and meets our need.

As I finish writing this devotional I am looking at circumstances that are not favorable to the completion of this book. I don't see how I can finish in time to meet my deadline. I do know that God has been there for me before when circumstances were threatening. I have been able to write more in less time during trials with God's help. He doesn't call us to do something and then leave us floundering. He is there to guide and direct us if we only ask.

Are you called to homeschool? Have you spent enough time with the Lord nurturing the only relationship that will empower you to do His will when in your flesh you see limitations that you think make God's call impossible?

PRAYER

Lord, at times I feel just like Moses. My weaknesses are many, and I don't believe I can fill Your call to homeschool. Please help me. ❧

FOOD FOR THOUGHT

1. What aspects of homeschooling are the most challenging for you? Have you cried out to the Lord for help in these areas?
2. Look for areas in the lives of your children where they feel like Moses and can't embrace God's call on their life. Share Exodus 4:10-12 with them.
3. Lay your weaknesses at the foot of the cross.

9

I HEARD WHAT YOU SAID, BUT WHAT DID YOU MEAN?

When thou sittest to eat with a ruler,
consider diligently what is before thee.

PROVERBS 23:1

❧

Often our family devotions include reading five Psalms and one chapter from Proverbs. Six-year-old Joanna asked what this verse meant, and I could see where she was heading with her question. She thought it meant that when you sit down to eat, you would use a ruler (like the one she uses for math) instead of a fork. She didn't know that a ruler could be a king, so she misunderstood the verse.

Sometimes we don't understand the words that others use when they speak to us. We easily confuse their communication when we are too embarrassed to ask for clarification. Joanna felt comfortable asking her question, even though we all laughed about the mix-up. Joanna laughed too. I might not be so willing to ask others to tell me what they mean if I thought they would laugh at me. Many of us fail to step out of our comfort zone and ask because it is easier to just act like we understand.

This is a mistake. Good communication between two people is based on a mutual understanding of what is being said. How we interpret words greatly affects their meaning to us. As our children develop communication skills, we must encourage them to ask questions when they do not understand. They need to develop a thirst for wisdom that will propel them past any fears they have about being laughed at for asking a dumb question. It helps to teach them how to laugh at themselves.

Joanna already knows these things. She asks questions all the time. She laughs easily if the answer is something obvious that she just missed. We have to be careful not to take advantage of her easygoing nature. More sensitive children need to be encouraged to ask questions. They will have a greater struggle if people laugh at them. I am glad that my children are in my home where I can be aware of these needs in their lives. How important it is to have good communication skills, and what better time is there to learn them than childhood.

How well are your family members communicating? Do you ask enough questions to be sure you understand what others mean?

PRAYER

Heavenly Father, we all have much to learn about communicating clearly one to another. Please help me to be a good model in this area. I pray that You would teach us how to work through our misunderstandings in a loving way. Thank You for children who feel free to ask questions. ❧

FOOD FOR THOUGHT

1. Take time when children are very young to observe their communication. Help them to express themselves clearly at an early age.
2. Set the example yourself by asking questions about Scripture. Don't be afraid to ask what you might think is a dumb question. There are no dumb questions when you are seeking to understand God's Word.
3. Do your children laugh at one another's misfortunes? Address this when they are young. While training them to lighten up and laugh at their own mistakes, warn them of the hurt that others experience when they are laughed at. This is a good time to teach about forgiveness too.

1 0

I HATE YOU

*For three things the earth is disquieted, and for four which
it cannot bear: . . . for an odious woman when she is married;
and an handmaid that is heir to her mistress.*

PROVERBS 30:21, 23

I haven't said "I hate you" often, but I have said it more than once. I have
said it to my husband in a moment of exasperation. It happens during those
times when he completely fails to understand me and in his ignorance says
and does things that make my life more difficult and leaves my emotions
damaged. It happens when I perceive him as not caring for me and I make my
husband the object of my disdain for my circumstances.

Oh, how misdirected my comment was each time I have said it. When I
say "I hate you" to my husband, I am rejecting the way he is treating me. I
am also telling God I hate Him and reject the circumstances He has allowed
for my growth. Obviously it is wrong to tell my husband I hate him, and there
are ways that I can keep from ever saying it again.

When Jim and I don't communicate well, typically I am misunderstood
and then criticized unjustly. My first response needs to be praise to the Lord.
I must express my gratefulness to God for allowing me to grow through trials. If I take the focus off of my husband immediately and seek God's direction in His gift to me—the trial—it is harder to develop a hatred for my
husband or God. The Bible makes it clear that "an odious woman when she

is married" is a problem. Odious women are filled with hatred. I don't want that to be me.

It is painful for a wife when a husband does not treat her well. Emotionally it can completely unravel a woman if she is not careful. Reacting with hurtful words does damage to her marriage and to her soul. Children don't see a godly role model in an odious mother. Eyes focused on a God who is good all of the time can mitigate the pain. Seeking to grow through trials can soften a hardening heart. Realizing that God allows problems for our own spiritual growth can help us to be more forgiving of others when they fail us.

Have you said any words that hurt lately? Deal with them right now.

PRAYER

Father, I don't like the trials You are using to grow my character lately. What You are requiring of me now is harder than it has been in the past. Forgive me for fighting Your plan and fighting with the people You are using in my life for Your glory. Help me to learn to embrace the pain of growth rather than to harden my heart toward others. ❧

FOOD FOR THOUGHT

1. Examine your life for wrong attitudes, actions, and words toward others. Are people or circumstances the biggest problem, or is your biggest problem how you are responding to the opportunities that God is giving to you so your character will grow?
2. Develop a mind-set of praise when trials come your way. Thank God for challenging people, and pray for those who hurt you.
3. Guard your soul from bitterness by refusing to be angry with people and circumstances that are difficult for you.

1 1

BE CAREFUL

Beware of false prophets, which come to you in sheep's clothing,
but inwardly they are ravening wolves.

MATTHEW 7:15

≈

When Julianne was two years old, she had two handfuls of white oval-shaped items. She eyed me with a look of suspicion. When I checked her hands, I discovered she was holding green bean seeds she had gotten into at the kitchen table. Fortunately she had not put any of these hard beans into her mouth. Julianne thought they were little mints like the candies her older sisters sometimes shared with her. She will look in drawers, go through purses, and do whatever else it takes to get a mint. Because the bean seeds looked like mints to her, she could easily have put them in her mouth and choked.

Sometimes what we see with our eyes appears to be something good for us when in actuality it can be quite harmful. As adults we have encountered this more than once. For our children it is different. They don't have the experience to discern good from evil very well. Young children do not think very deeply about what they see. Often what they see is filtered through a tiny frame of reference.

When Julianne got into trouble with the bean seeds, she was only familiar with one kind of mint and knew its shape. To her, the seeds must be mints. Her older brothers and sisters probably would have spotted the difference right away. Obviously we want to prevent our young children from harm, but what about the older children? We need to protect them too. Even young adults who may have maturity beyond their years still haven't lived long enough to develop the wisdom that older adults can offer.

On occasion I find myself watching my younger children closely while figuring that my older children already "know better." In some areas they do, but growing up involves gaining understanding and wisdom in all areas. Young adults can be very trusting in their relationships until they have a few bad experiences. We should teach them to be careful in their relationships. Advise them not to share too deeply with someone they have just met. It seems clear to us why not, but they may not see the potential harm because they have no experience with people who are wolves in sheep's clothing.

Recently I had a challenging experience with someone that made my girls uncomfortable. They tried to tell me, but I said they were misunderstanding the person. Eventually some issues surfaced, and I saw my daughters had read the person accurately. I praised them and promised to seek their input in the future since they saw what I did not. My example will encourage them to do the same with me.

Are you training your children to be discerning?

PRAYER

Heavenly Father, I thank You that You have asked me to train my children at home. We are blessed by how much time we have to talk about so many things. Keep me mindful of their need to learn to look critically at situations and people, that they might learn to discern evil while they are yet young. ❧

FOOD FOR THOUGHT

1. Study Matthew 7:15 with your children, and be sure they understand what it means.
2. Encourage your children to be discerning by asking questions when they have concerns about people or situations.
3. Humble yourself and let them show you what you miss.

12

WEAK FLESH

Watch ye and pray, lest ye enter into temptation.
The spirit truly is ready, but the flesh is weak.

MARK 14:38

༝ॐ

*M*y oldest three children were at piano lessons, and I was writing upstairs. Jim was working on school with our two-, three-, five-, and seven-year-olds. I came downstairs, and he made the comment, "I think I might be able to handle four kids." We have seven! We believe children are a blessing, and in no way do I want to imply we have too many. The problem isn't them—it's us.

I had a vague idea what this verse meant before I had children and began homeschooling. Now I *know* what it means! My heart can be in the right place and my plans all made, but I don't always have the energy to execute my plans. Just when I feel like I can juggle everything successfully, something new enters my life and throws me off again. This is not a result of poor planning, but rather providential training for me from God. Every time I feel confident in my own abilities, I tend not to seek God. I rely on myself.

God wants us to rely solely on Him for our provision. If you feel like you can't handle what is before you, that's good. Our flesh is too weak to do what God desires for us. Only when we reach for His grace do we have what it takes to get our jobs done. I am glad that God keeps me one step outside of my comfort zone. It is in this place that I seek Him the most. It does not hurt to keep your children reaching out in front of them too. Once we relax and get comfortable with our surroundings, the growth in our life rapidly slows down. Conversely, if you keep reaching out for what God has next, growth often speeds up.

Some mothers stop homeschooling when their children enter high school. This is fine if it is for the right reasons. If it is because you are burned-out and have nothing left to give, there may be a better alternative. I have found the high school years to be a blessed time of fruit-bearing. I would not want to miss this. Our flesh is weak. We can't change this, but we can reach out to God to give us exactly what we need to do the work He has called us to do.

Are you trying to homeschool by yourself, or are you crying out for God's grace daily?

PRAYER

Father, thank You for taking me out of my comfort zone. I can see how weak my flesh is and why I need to seek You for my strength. For years I relied on my own abilities without seeking Your grace. It is much easier now that I look to You instead of to myself. Thank You for showing me this truth. ❧

FOOD FOR THOUGHT

1. Make a list of all your abilities that are helpful to you as you homeschool. Do you focus on these rather than on God's grace?
2. Assess the abilities of your children, and teach them to ask God to help them use these abilities for His glory.
3. Rejoice in knowing how valuable this teaching is for your children to receive in their youth.

13

I LOVE YOU

My little children, let us not love in word, neither in tongue; but in deed and in truth.

1 JOHN 3:18

⊶⅋

*A*s Jamie's fourteenth birthday approached, our relationship with her was not as strong as it had been in times past. She was having trouble following directions and had a sour attitude. It seemed that even the small requirements we made of her were too much. She had given up. She didn't feel loved. This problem had developed over time, but we just missed it.

Of course Jim and I love her very much, but our continuing frustration with her behavior and her attitude did little to communicate love. We were unknowingly loving conditionally. As long as she did what she was supposed to do, everything was fine. But when there were problems, small issues got bigger because she did not feel we loved her for who she was—only for what she did or did not do. In my zeal to train her properly, I corrected her more than I praised her. That had disastrous results.

Jamie is our firstborn. Firstborns have some common characteristics. They tend to be leaders, take a lot of responsibility, and want things done a certain way. Everyone depends on them. Homeschool moms have to pay close attention to how much they depend on their firstborn. It is good to require our children to work, but the firstborn can easily end up shouldering too much of the load. We can get comfortable with their skills and fail to allow the next children to learn to develop those same skills.

But it is important that we keep promoting our oldest child. Just yesterday Jenny (age twelve) asked me if she could do more of the cooking. She mentioned that Jamie had been doing it for a long time. She is right. I get complacent about our meals because Jamie takes care of them. It is now Jenny's turn, and Jamie will have new areas to learn. Jamie is proficient in the kitchen and should expand her horizons. Our love for her is not a function of her productivity, but of who she is in our family. In offering her more opportunities because she has been faithful in the small things (kitchen service) we hope that our love for her will continue to motivate her on to good works.

Do your children really know that you love them? Do you have any strings attached?

PRAYER

Dear God, forgive us for loving conditionally. Our children are in process, and we forget that they are still children. Help us to communicate clearly that their worth is in who they are, not in what they do. Teach us how to correct them in love. Show us how to motivate them by our love. Help us to please You. ❧

FOOD FOR THOUGHT

1. How is your relationship with your firstborn? Are you too hard on him or her? Do you expect more from him or her than you should?
2. Periodically ask your children if they feel loved. Hold yourself accountable to them, so that any problems in this area can be addressed quickly.
3. Read Gary Chapman's series on The Five Love Languages to help you learn how to communicate love to your spouse, teenagers, and children.

14

I HAD TO WAIT

Wait on the LORD: be of good courage, and he shall strengthen thine heart: wait, I say, on the LORD.

PSALM 27:14

*I*t seemed to me that my husband's independent spirit would never change. While I desired oneness in our marriage, it seemed he was comfortable making decisions on his own. This particularly bothered me in the area of finances. Money was in short supply for home improvements but was available for farm implements. While I sought his opinion on purchases that I made beyond our budget, he was taking on more and more farm machinery without discussing it with me, and I felt left out of our relationship.

One Saturday morning Jim had planned to attend an auction in a nearby town. They were selling a planter that he wanted. Jim told me he would be going and that he thought it would cost about $100. The day of the auction I woke up heavy of heart. I realized we had not talked together about this purchase and the timing of it (right before Christmas). I nicely brought up my concern to him that he just announced his intentions without discussing them with me.

What a response I received! He humbly and repeatedly apologized for leaving me out. He had not intended this but got absorbed in what he was doing, forgetting everything else. That is just the way he operates. For many years I had interpreted this as an independent spirit and reacted to it. If I am not careful I can fall into this pattern now. When I react in the wrong way to his perceived independence, he becomes defensive and has even less desire for oneness in our marriage.

A man does not need to get approval from his wife for all of his purchases. But there is something special that happens in a marriage when a husband asks his wife for her opinion. I had to wait a long time for God to work in Jim's heart and in my own so that we would relate properly in this area. We still get challenged, but if I respond kindly to Jim, he is more apt to discuss the matter with me. I am glad that I waited for God to reveal to me what I needed to know rather than hardening my heart against my husband. I misunderstood Jim's actions and can deal with it differently now that I know his heart.

Are you facing something challenging in your life and God is requiring you to wait on Him for an answer? Thank Him for developing in you the character quality of patience.

PRAYER

Lord, You know that I don't like to wait. I want the answer NOW! Waiting can be long and painful, but I know that the timing of our waiting is allowed by You so that You can work Your good purposes in us. Thank You that the trials and tribulations of life will teach us patience if only we will let them. ❧

FOOD FOR THOUGHT

1. Do you have relationship problems? Is God teaching you to wait?
2. Treat yourself to the Bible study *The Fruit of the Spirit Is Patience* by Lynn Stanley.
3. Remember to pray regularly for those areas in your life where God is calling you to wait. Don't pray for others to change, but that patience would be developed in you during the time of waiting.

15

WHY DO I NEED A DENIM JUMPER?

*Whose adorning let it not be that outward adorning of plaiting
the hair, and of wearing of gold, or of putting on of apparel;
but let it be the hidden man of the heart, in that which is not
corruptible, even the ornament of a meek and quiet spirit,
which is in the sight of God of great price.*

1 PETER 3:3-4

◦§

*T*welve years ago when we started to homeschool our children I was looking for direction so I could do it "right." The first few years I observed, read,
and studied to find out what I should be doing. It was about this time that our
conviction to dress modestly was forcing me to figure out what dressing modestly really looked like.

Each family goes through the process of deciding what is appropriate and
what is not. My only frame of reference regarding modest clothing at that time
was homeschool families. I observed the mothers and daughters wearing
denim jumpers frequently. Their practicality in the home attracted me, so I set
out to find some. They were hard to locate at stores, so I ended up doing some
sewing.

Pregnancy and nursing worked well in denim jumpers. So I settled into
these as the focus of my wardrobe. I bought every one I found at garage
sales and over time built up a good supply. I wore some of them out and eventually could find what I wanted in stores at an affordable price. Then some-

thing happened. I started to think that somehow wearing these jumpers would make me a better homeschool mom. I subconsciously began to associate what I was wearing with success in homeschooling.

I like denim jumpers. They are comfortable. But they are not the focus of my wardrobe anymore. I realized that in my quest to learn how to homeschool, I was looking at externals. While modest clothing is important, it is not defined as only a denim jumper. I had to look beyond this "uniform" of the homeschool mom and seek the deeper issues of the heart. Developing the fruits of the Spirit, particularly patience, will help me to be a better homeschool mom. Pruning the dead wood in my life will help me more than wearing a certain type of dress. I have to look to the Lord for my direction, not to what other homeschoolers around me look like.

Are you relying on externals to get you through?

PRAYER

Dear Lord, thank You for the examples You brought to my path in the early years of homeschooling that helped point me in the right direction. Thank You for the opportunity to mature into the important matters of the heart. Please continue to show me what is truly important so I can put my focus there. ❧

FOOD FOR THOUGHT

1. Are you looking at other homeschool families to show you what a homeschooling family should look like? Be careful! God has not called all of us to look the same.

2. List the strengths you have in your own family, and think about ways these strengths can encourage others. Focus on heart issues rather than externals.

3. Are there any special trademarks you have developed in your family that are unique? Consider the image you have as a family and whether it is yours and not just a copy of someone else's. Let God direct your steps rather than the expectations of man.

1 6

TOO MANY TEARS

They that sow in tears shall reap in joy. He the goeth forth and weepeth, bearing precious seed, shall doubtless come again with rejoicing, bringing his sheaves with him.

PSALM 126:5-6

It seems I cry too much lately. I used to think tears meant something was wrong that needed to be fixed. Now I know that in some seasons of life the process of sowing is so intense that I feel I can hardly go on. Raising children is demanding business. Meeting the needs of all ages, toddlers through teens, can be overwhelming even in the best of circumstances. Factor in a strained marital relationship, a husband working two jobs, and a lonely wife and mother and you can see how the challenges mount.

Circumstances that seem like more than we can bear can bring us to tears. We may bring these circumstances upon ourselves, but often tough times are just a part of the building process. The tears that accompany these times of sowing will yield future reaping in joy, the Bible assures us. Maybe crying isn't such a bad thing after all. If tears release stress and help you to go on, they can be beneficial. This is a superior alternative to the anger that can surface during the intense times.

Modern farming equipment makes it look as though sowing seed is pretty easy. When seed was sown by hand, it was quite a lot of work. But it was done because the farmer was preparing for a harvest and would not have one unless he sowed seed. Many obstacles had to be overcome to get the seed sown. There are obstacles in our lives as we sow. These obstacles will not prevent us from sowing if we keep our focus on the future benefit that comes from what we sow now. We must not give up.

Some seasons of life are especially difficult. The work is hard, and there is little feedback. These times of intense seed sowing are the seasons of investing in our children. The dividends that will come from training our children in the way they should go will be more than we can count. With a vision for the future joy, we can hang on in our present tearful times. The harvest will come as we are faithful in the planting.

Do you feel like you cry too often about too many things? Me too!

PRAYER

Dear God, I desperately need Your perspective on my circumstances. I don't see how I can get through the grind of some days. I struggle with handling the intensity of training so many children for You. I feel like a crybaby when I end up weeping when the going gets tough. Help me to remember that sowing in tears is followed by reaping in joy. Help me to keep this perspective throughout our homeschooling journey. ❧

FOOD FOR THOUGHT

1. Have you considered how much work you are doing to train your children properly? Ponder the magnitude of the task, and give yourself a break—cry if you need to.
2. Develop a vision for the future of each of your children. Motivate yourself by thinking about how much strengthening their weak areas in their youth will help them all of their lives.
3. Realize that the fruit produced in your children now will live on long after you are gone from this earth. What a legacy!

17

YOU DIDN'T DO . . .

*And why beholdest thou the mote that is in thy brother's eye,
but perceivest not the beam that is in thine own eye?*

LUKE 6:41

❧

Jim has invested a lot of money in beekeeping equipment. Since we moved to our farm three years ago, he hasn't been able to set up his honey bottling area and therefore hasn't gotten any bees yet. The equipment has just been sitting, and we have not been able to benefit from the income that we were previously receiving from his beekeeping venture. Periodically it bothers me to think about this wasted potential. He will get to it eventually, but other priorities have been more important.

I have been critical of this until tonight. I was refilling a half-gallon jar with dried pinto beans from our food storage. I looked around at the plentiful varieties of dried beans, legumes, and rice that I have not taken the time to prepare very often since we have moved. Other things have crowded out the time for it. I am guilty of the same thing that Jim is doing. I am not utilizing what we already have for the benefit of our family. I need to make this a priority as much as Jim needs to get his beekeeping going again.

We must be careful as we correct our children not to do it with a critical spirit. Character issues in their life can be the same as the character issues in our own lives. If we are not open and honest with them about our areas of struggle, we can be seen by them as criticizing them for doing the very thing that we are also doing. Until we humble ourselves it will be difficult to have much impact on our children. Isn't our bad example often the reason they end up with some of their character problems in the first place?

You can see that we really have no choice but to clean up the areas of our life that are not what they should be. Perfection is not the goal, but a sweet spirit during the process models for our children what they need to do too. A sweet spirit crowds out a critical spirit. A sweet spirit is easily listened to. Our children need us. They need us to teach them what is right. We must learn to talk to them in ways that draw them closer to us rather than push them away.

Are you guilty of the same thing that you criticize someone else for doing? Ouch!

PRAYER

Father, I really struggle with a critical spirit. I don't mean for it to happen, but I haven't yet learned how to correct with a sweet spirit. I need Your help to learn how to do this in a manner pleasing to You. Please forgive me for judging my husband for the same problem I have myself. Thank You for Your grace. ❧

FOOD FOR THOUGHT

1. Define a critical spirit. Does anyone in your family have a critical spirit? Begin to address this immediately.
2. Define humility. Can you be humble about your own weak areas in front of your family? This is the first step toward correcting with a sweet spirit.
3. Praise God for all of the character growth that homeschooling brings to your life personally.

18

MUSIC LESSONS

Sing unto him a new song; play skillfully with a loud noise.

PSALM 33:3

✑

So far our two oldest daughters and oldest son have taken piano lessons. Lessons and practice have not always been their favorite pursuits. My son doesn't like piano, but that's okay. As parents we don't lay foundations for our children to make them happy. We lay them to give our children the building blocks for their future.

Psalm 33 indicates that one way we can express our joy and praise to the Lord is through skillful playing. Piano lessons teach our children how to play the piano, and practicing develops their skill. Once developed, this ability is theirs to use to honor the Lord. It is also a prerequisite in our family if they want to learn to play another instrument. While they are young they may not yet be able to see the value in developing such a skill. If we cater only to what they like to do, we miss the opportunity for them to benefit from our vision.

As an adult I can see the value in having an understanding of notes, scales, and music in general. I have wished a number of times that I could play the piano. As a child I had no clue about the value in this, nor was I even interested. One of the girls is particularly gifted in piano, which she would not have discovered if we had not encouraged her in the early days to keep practicing. I want my children to have this opportunity available to them now since adult life doesn't lend itself to learning to play an instrument quite like childhood does.

We must make wise choices in the selection of extra activities for our children. If we are alert to the Scriptures, we can see biblical guidelines for deciding which activities are most profitable. If we instead merely fuel their appetites for what they like to do, we may not be encouraging them to do what is best. Children haven't lived long enough to know what is important to their future. That's why parents can bless them so richly by requiring them to do things that will be good for them even if they don't like it.

Are you letting your children direct their life by their preferences, or are you requiring some things that are not their favorite choices?

PRAYER

Lord, thank You for my husband's wisdom in requiring each of our children to take piano lessons as a music foundation. I pray that they would appreciate the opportunity even if it is not their preference. Thank You for giving us wisdom as parents to seek opportunities for our children that will enhance their future. Continue to guide us as we make decisions about activities for each of our children in the future. ⇔

FOOD FOR THOUGHT

1. Take inventory of the activities that your children are involved in. Evaluate them in terms of how these activities prepare them for future adult life. Are there any additions or deletions that you need to make in their activity selections?
2. Do you have criteria to use to determine if an activity will be a good choice for your family? Examples might include cost, time, level of commitment, individual or family focus, etc.
3. Encourage your children that they can enjoy activities that are not their preference when they develop a right attitude toward what you are requiring of them.

1 9

GOD DOES THE TESTING

*My brethren, be not many masters [teachers], knowing that
we shall receive the greater condemnation.*

JAMES 3:1

I liked to get good grades in school. In fact, I liked to get the best grades. A perfect paper gave me the satisfaction that I had done a good job. I had passed the test with flying colors. God gives us tests all the time. He wants to see if we really believe as we say we do. God's tests are often difficult, and even though I think I know the answers, my actions prove otherwise. I often confuse God's tests for Satan's attacks.

I feel defeated when I sense that I have allowed Satan to control me because of my sin. If I would look at challenges as God's tests, I would be more motivated to do what's right. The difference between tests and attacks can be so subtle I don't necessarily assess them correctly. Wouldn't it be nice if there were some sort of caller ID to solve this problem?

Actually it is easier to view everything as God testing us to see if we are applying what we know. As I write more and speak to more women at conferences, mothers' brunches, etc., I am seeing that as a teacher I am indeed tested in the very areas in which I teach. Where before I used to look at situations and think that Satan was out to mess something up, now I am more apt to see that God is giving me opportunities to choose correctly. Trials feel like final exams in character growth. How will I respond?

I still like to pass tests. But God's tests are the ones that really matter. Whenever I am tempted to respond incorrectly to my surroundings, I am aware that I can pass or fail the test right at that point. Instead of seeking the perfect grade, I am looking for improvement. Any time I respond better to a situation than I might have in the past, I feel like I am passing the test. Homeschoolers don't tend to give a lot of tests. But it may be an advantage to teach our children about how God tests us when we have learned a new truth. Soon after learning truth we are tested to see if we will apply what we have learned. This is the best test we can prepare our children to pass in their lifetimes.

Is God testing you? Are you passing?

PRAYER

Lord, please forgive me for blaming so much on Satan. He is the enemy of truth, but I can't blame my failures on him. Thank You for testing me so often. That helps me to see where I need to study more. It shows me when I haven't understood the material at all. I pray for understanding and wisdom, that I might pass more and more tests in the future. I want my life to bring glory to You. ❧

FOOD FOR THOUGHT

1. Think of James 3:1 in terms of your role as teacher to your children. Particularly in the area of character, do you see God bringing trials to test you after you communicate truths to your children? Let this be a motivation to get a passing grade.
2. We don't always pass God's tests. Ask forgiveness when you realize He gave you the opportunity to choose wisely but you did not.
3. Pray for wisdom in applying God's truth.

2 0

PULL WEEDS EARLY

But exhort one another daily, while it is called Today;
lest any of you be hardened through the deceitfulness of sin.

HEBREWS 3:13

&

We enjoy a fruitful garden. Ordering and planting seeds and plants usually goes well. The problem is the weeds. Oh, for a while the garden looks fine, and our vegetables begin to poke through the ground. We can see the new growth. But along with the vegetable plants come the tiny weeds. If the weeds are pulled out early, while they are still small, the project is rather simple. But if left to grow, these weeds begin to grow faster than the vegetables. They can easily overshadow and actually kill the good plants.

Sin is just like the weeds in the garden. It starts out small and seemingly insignificant. If you fail to address sin when it is first identified, it grows. Sometimes it grows so big that it looks impossible to deal with at all. The spiritual growth in your life is dwarfed by such sin. It would be easy to throw your hands up at this point and just give up.

That's how our garden looked this year—impossible. Some weeds were between three and four feet tall. I couldn't even see the tomato plants. I suggested we go at it with the lawnmower! But my husband and children spent some time weeding it, and there were the tomato plants! The green pepper plants were okay too. It took some time to tackle the huge weeds, but they were able to salvage some of the garden.

Sin that is denied in your life can be dealt with later, but it is much harder after you have allowed it to grow. When sin is addressed in its infancy, it can be easier to eradicate. How important it is for us as parents to exhort our children daily so that sin is dealt with promptly. If children harden their hearts over time, it is much more difficult to correct the problems, and they can do significant damage to their lives in the process. There is a difference between right and wrong. Keep their hearts tender toward what is right, and you won't have four-foot-high weeds in their lives that need to be pulled.

Are you overlooking sin in your life or in the lives of your children? Face it now, and fix it before it grows out of control.

PRAYER

Heavenly Father, thank You for the accountability that I have with my family. They can point out sin in my life that I might overlook. Help me to be open to their observations. Forgive me for pride that prevents me from accepting their concerns. Help us all learn to exhort one another daily. Let us be an encouragement to each other when we are struggling. Show us what needs to be weeded out of our lives early before the weeds get too big. ✦

FOOD FOR THOUGHT

1. Meditate on how creation teaches us about God's natural laws. Remember the results produced by the unweeded garden.
2. Grow a garden, and use it to illustrate this powerful truth to your children. Let them get their hands dirty!
3. Humble yourself to a trusted friend, and see if there are any blind spots in your life where sin has gone undetected. Be prepared for a fruitful garden in your life when you deal with sin quickly.

21

PLEASE DON'T

For the wrath of man worketh not the righteousness of God.

JAMES 1:20

❧

Two-year-old Julianne loves taking a bath. She likes to fill the tub with toys and play with the washcloth. One time she took a bar of soap and started washing her body with it. I told her not to touch her eyes because the soap would make them sting. A minute or two later she rubbed her eyes and then began to cry. I was surprised that she did exactly what I warned her would bring her harm.

I don't believe in this case that she was disobeying me. I think she really did not understand my warning. There are negative commands in the Bible that tell us not to do certain things. We need to study the Bible so that we understand the warnings. Once we understand the warnings, we need to follow them. There are many verses that warn us about anger. This verse in James is straightforward. It says that the anger of man does not work God's righteousness. It makes sense, but how many of us, knowing this truth, still get angry about the wrong things or for the wrong reasons?

We don't seem to understand the warning here. If we sin in our anger, the results will always be poor. Our anger cannot work the righteousness of God because we are not God. God's wrath can't be our wrath. Knowing these things and putting them into practice are not the same. Homeschool days can be long and tedious. Many opportunities to become angry can come in a single day. If we heed the warning in James, we will not become angry. If we are angry, then we have not benefited from the warning and will pay the price, much like Julianne did when she rubbed soap in her eyes.

God has good reasons for telling us not to do some things—they are harmful to us. But the warnings only help when we heed them. Reading Scripture must translate into a change in behavior when we see the light. Old habits die hard, but they must die. Whatever it takes to correct a problem area is worth the effort. God's Word is true and accurate. It is there to help us when we seek answers to our questions in the Bible.

Are you failing to heed a warning that you have read in the Bible? Follow it now.

PRAYER

Dear Jesus, I feel as though I have a learning disorder. I read Your Word, but I see that I don't follow it so well. I know what is right, but I still do what is wrong. Particularly in the area of anger, I understand that I should not be angry but have not gotten victory in this area yet. Thank You for the improvement, but help me to rid sinful anger from my life once and for all. Help me to be sweet and gentle in all the circumstances of life. May my life be a testimony to Your grace. ❧

FOOD FOR THOUGHT

1. Get a cassette or video of "Freedom from the Spirit of Anger" by Dr. S. M. Davis (order at 1-800-500-8853).
2. Memorize James 1:20.
3. Consider the purpose of warnings in the Bible. Are there any that stand out to you? Are you following them?

22

RESPOND PROPERLY

The heart of the righteous studieth to answer:
but the mouth of the wicked poureth out evil things.

PROVERBS 15:28

⋄

I am amazed by how many situations occur each day in the relationships between family members. Imagine the challenges that may come to a family of nine living under the same roof trying to get along with each other during twelve to fourteen hours together each day. The youngest ones are just learning how to get along with others. This means they get along one minute and don't the next. The older ones know how to push each other's buttons. This means they bicker. Dad and Mom don't always understand each other. This means that Mom can be frustrated and lonely, while Dad is wondering what is wrong.

It sounds like a mess, and it is when interpersonal conflicts are not managed well. As a mom, I tend to jump in too often and try to settle the differences. This can be appropriate. Swift and decisive action is often necessary with young children. Older ones have more complicated issues that take more thought on our part if we are to handle them effectively. We can offer insight to the older ones, but they need to learn to work through their own relationships. Notice where this verse tells us to do our thinking.

It says "the heart of the righteous studieth to answer." I use my mind to think. Sometimes the connection between my mind and my tongue is so short that I say words I regret. I don't study my answer long enough before I speak, and what pours out is evil. This verse says that the wicked pour evil out of their mouths. No homeschooling mother wants to be put in this category!

Our heart is the place to ponder our answer. The heart is deep. It is not superficial. Thinking through a matter in our heart slows our response time with our tongue. When we do speak after studying our response in our heart, we are more likely to respond correctly. It may seem overwhelming to approach relationships this way, but the alternative is to have our mouths pour out evil things. Which way would you rather have it?

Do you answer right away without studying how to answer?

PRAYER

Father, teach me how to be quick to listen and slow to speak. Help me to study my answers in my heart instead of saying what comes off the top of my head. Please help our family learn to respond correctly to each other throughout the day. Homeschooling is the perfect environment for relationship training, and I want to teach them what is right. Once again, help me to do a better job of modeling right responses to my family. ❧

FOOD FOR THOUGHT

1. Realize that character training is a part of the curriculum and should not be overlooked. Don't ignore relationship problems in favor of getting the book work done. Teach your children how to get along well with each other.
2. Praise any improvement that you see in relationships in your family. Be an encourager as your children learn godly character. Be open about your own character growth, and give them a realistic idea of how long this takes.
3. Aren't you glad you are with your children so much that you can see the needs in this area?

2 3

GOD'S WILL

*Jesus saith unto them, My meat is to do the will of him
that sent me, and to finish his work.*

JOHN 4:34

❧

On the day that I finally surrendered my will to God's call on my life to
write and speak to women, I was pondering the magnitude of the work
before me. In less than three years I had two books published, and the
requests for me to speak were on the increase. I had not marketed myself
as a speaker, so that we would know it was God who was opening the
doors. For four years I wrestled with the whole concept. I was happy to be
a stay-at-home mom, and I wasn't sure I could handle the pressure these new
responsibilities would bring.

Many people ask me how I do it all. I don't have an answer other than
the grace of God. Just thinking about how I homeschool seven children,
live on a ten-acre farm, and write and speak makes me tired. There is no
way my flesh can do all of this, even if I am organized. But I have noticed
great blessing in following God's will. I can write in much less time than
seems normal to me. It is as if God allows me to do more in less time. I
have experienced this before.

I also notice that God shows me truths when I am in the middle of doing
something with the children. One day I was helping a friend of mine by
proofreading a manuscript her son had written. We talked awhile, and I gave

my input. I liked much of what I saw, but some key points were missing. Later in the day, while washing out paintbrushes for Joanna and Josiah, God showed me a powerful addition that could pull the book together for my friend's son. I saw that as I filled my role as Mom, God could still fill my mind with what I needed without having to spend a lot of time working on it.

I have repeatedly seen that when I am in God's will, He helps me in a supernatural way to accomplish what He asks of me. We homeschool moms go through times when we can't see any way we can continue to home-school. It may be disorganization, child training issues, or just the sheer volume of work that weighs us down. Whatever the cause, the answer is still found in our purpose to follow God's will and to finish what He has called us to do. Resting in God's power gives us the ability to do extraordinary things for Him.

Are you unsure about whether you can homeschool? Don't worry—if it is God's will, then you can, with His help.

PRAYER

Dear God, I thank You for showing me Your desires for me. Forgive me for fighting You so long in my ignorance. I thought I had to juggle it all and make it work. Now I understand that You will enable me to do amazing things when I am in Your will. Thank You! ๛

FOOD FOR THOUGHT

1. Have you considered that as a homeschool mom you are putty in God's hands? Have you allowed Him to shape you for the task?
2. Reflect back on times when you did things that now seem beyond comprehension. Was this because God was helping you?
3. Can you trust God with your homeschooling efforts?

24

SHE WAS AFRAID

What time I am afraid, I will trust in thee.

PSALM 56:3

❧

Our children love it when we go through the drive-through car wash. Because it is a rare occurrence, they view it as a special treat. Everyone does not enjoy the car wash though. At two years old Julianne had no concept of what the car wash was all about. As the other children laughed and made delighted squeals, Julianne was very serious. Gradually a look of terror came to her face. The water, the brushes, and the air dryer all were frightening to her. She had no idea what was happening to her because of her limited frame of reference.

As a middle-aged mom, I see that there are many experiences in life I have not had yet. Before I do something for the first time, I can become fearful of the unknown. Not knowing what to expect can make me uneasy. My fears aren't like little Julianne's in the car wash though. She was afraid of the unknown because her experiences were so limited. I am fearful of what could happen because so many life experiences have taught me to be careful. Once optimistically jumping into new situations with both feet, I am now cautious because I know of the dangers that are out there.

I can fear my own inadequacy. I have listened to myself say the words "I can't do this" too often. The solution to fear, be it fear of what is happening around us or fears about ourselves, is to trust God. Life teaches us that many of our fears are unwarranted. Often what we fear doesn't ever happen. Does God protect us from what we fear? Sometimes, but not always. But when our fears come true, He is there to walk us through the terror if we trust in Him.

After enduring five miscarriages in eighteen months, I was afraid. While desiring to welcome all of the children God would give us, I was confused by what was happening to me. My frame of reference is too small to understand God in this matter. In attempting to deal with my fear, I saw that until I released it to God and accepted the possibility of another miscarriage, I would be controlled by my fear. Guess what? I placed my trust in God, and the fear is gone. If these miscarriages are a part of following what we believe is God's will for us in trusting Him for our family size, then I have to trust Him completely in the whole thing.

Are you afraid of anything right now? Don't hide behind it. Get it out in the open so you can see it, and release it to God whom you can trust when you are afraid.

PRAYER

Dear Lord, I rejoice in Your presence when I am afraid. I have felt peace after releasing my fears to You. May my testimony be an encouragement to my family. ❧

FOOD FOR THOUGHT

1. What makes you afraid? Are you trying to deal with it yourself, or have you placed your fear at the altar where it belongs?
2. Memorize Psalm 56:3 with your children.
3. Are you afraid to start homeschooling because of the unknown? Are you afraid to continue homeschooling because you know what it requires of you? God is where you should put your trust!

2 5

I GOT CAUGHT

for the wisdom of this world is foolishness with God. for it is written,
He taketh the wise in their own craftiness. And again,
The Lord knoweth the thoughts of the wise, that they are vain.

1 CORINTHIANS 3:19-20

I rarely sneak a candy bar. It isn't good for me, and I don't usually eat between meals. One night I was having a terrible time with the munchies. I had a few potato chips with dip, which was bad enough, but I was still hungry. I remembered the Snickers bars we had in the freezer to use in a fruit salad.

For some reason I decided to eat a Snickers bar secretly before the children had gone to bed. What an example! It wasn't easy to do since the children tend to hover around me. I got the candy bar out of the freezer, and then as I was about to pour a glass of milk, a child entered the kitchen. I casually covered the candy bar with a bowl on the counter while I poured my milk. I, with milk and candy bar, slipped away to our schoolroom and sat by myself on the couch in the dark. I guess you could say I was hiding. I took my first bite, enjoying this treat, when seven-year-old Jonathan sat down on the other end of the couch.

Still in the dark I hid my candy bar behind my glass of milk so as not to be discovered as Jonathan talked to me. After a couple of minutes I took another bite. Jonathan strained to see what I was eating in the dark. He could not see very well and then asked me, "Mom, are you eating a glue stick?" I couldn't cover my folly any longer as I burst out laughing. My son had found me out.

God does too. We think we can hide from Him, but how can you hide from Someone who is everywhere all of the time? I can manage to slip away from the children for a minute or two here and there, but God is always with me. He sees me *and* knows my thoughts. We get complacent because when we keep our thoughts to ourselves, the people around us don't know anything about them. God knows all the time. There is not one thought that I have that I can hide from Him. It seems prudent that I should not even try to hide anything from God. He will find me out more quickly than Jonathan did.

Are you hiding something from God? You only think you are because He already knows.

PRAYER

Lord, how I forget that You know my thoughts. How often my thoughts are displeasing to You. Help me to do what is right without sneaking around trying to hide what is wrong in my life. I pray that You would bring the areas of my life that need to be addressed right to the surface. I can't hide from You anyway. ❧

FOOD FOR THOUGHT

1. Do you harbor any wrong attitudes in your mind that you think nobody knows about? God does.
2. Do your children sneak food? Use this as a training tool to help them see that they must do what is right in God's eyes since He sees it all.
3. Humble yourself, and be a good example to your children.

2 6

WORDS CAN HURT

Let no corrupt communication proceed out of your mouth, but that which is good to the use of edifying, that it may minister grace unto the hearers.

EPHESIANS 4:29

One evening as I was leaving to pick up my two oldest daughters from a drama class, I was surprised to hear a shrieking kitten as my foot landed on top of it. When I looked down, it was nowhere to be found. The two other kittens were sitting on the stairs looking at me. As I drove away I prayed that the kitten was okay and would be back on the steps when I returned. All of the way to the class I was troubled about injuring that poor little innocent kitten. Then it dawned on me that when I lash out verbally at my children, the damage is far greater than what happened to the kitten.

We may unintentionally care more about the physical harm that we accidentally do to an animal than about the tremendous emotional damage that we do with wrong speech. The childhood taunt that "sticks and stones will break my bones, but words will never hurt me" is out-and-out untrue. We may very well recover more quickly from broken bones than we do from harmful words, especially when they are spoken by those who are close to us. Imagine the responsibility we have to train our children to speak appropriately to us and to their siblings considering how many hours a day we spend together.

Not one single day goes by that I am not dealing with "corrupt communication" from at least one member of the family. Learning to speak only what is edifying to others is a formidable task. It is harder for the children when Dad and Mom don't provide a good role model. Teasing and sarcasm have no place in our homes. Neither of them are edifying, and both should be eliminated. Though this cancer is widely accepted as normal in our culture, we need to prevent it from growing in our family. If teasing and sarcasm are allowed between siblings in their youth, it will be very difficult to break that bad habit in adulthood.

I get exhausted dealing with so many children who need to reexamine their speech. I feel I repeat myself constantly in this area. But I will continue to do so until we get it right. They so naturally will say derogatory things to each other that I must be vigilant to train them in the godly pursuit of edifying speech. This is all done while I am learning the same thing alongside them.

How do your children speak to each other? To you?

PRAYER

Heavenly Father, I confess that I have not been the best example of edifying speech. My words hurt, and I need Your help to do a better job. I pray for insight into ways to teach my children to speak properly to one another as a foundation for all of their future relationships. Please help me with this big job. ❧

FOOD FOR THOUGHT

1. Have you asked your children lately how your words are affecting them? Humbly do so, prepared to apologize.
2. Set the tone in your home by doing exactly what you want to teach your children. Only say what is good and useful for edifying and ministering grace.
3. Discover how to correct children while following the command in this verse.

2 7

REDEEM THE TIME

Walk in wisdom toward them that are without, redeeming the time.

COLOSSIANS 4:5

❧

*T*here doesn't ever seem to be enough time anymore. I still remember having a lot of time on my hands as a child. I wish I could get that time back because now I see how I could have used it better. Once time is gone, you cannot get it back—ever. My children have a limited amount of time in their youth to prepare for adult life. I want them to redeem this time because it passes quickly, and this unique opportunity to prepare for life does not come again.

How to spend time wisely is a challenge we face throughout all of our years. It must be answered individually. It should be given some thought. Children are not usually born good time managers. They need to be trained in how to set priorities, eliminate the unnecessary, and use time productively. The activities and pursuits that we allow or encourage in their youth affect their time management skills as adults.

The sports culture in our country is addictive. There seems to be a pull in some homeschooling families to take on an organized sport or two for each child. I heard a homeschool mother of eight speak at a conference where she shared how each of her children were in a baseball league, and one Saturday all of her children had games on different fields. She handed her husband a schedule as she left for the games in another car as they began a

---

day of playing shuttle bus. The number of games they had in that one day was staggering.

Sports are not bad. We have bats, balls, and bases in our home. But they do not direct our schedule. Sports don't necessarily do much to prepare children for life. If sports leagues nurtured a desire in youth to exercise throughout their whole life, they might fit our goal. But rather it seems that many men spend hours in front of the television watching sports without any desire to exercise themselves. How much better would it be for our young boys to learn godly character and service that would serve them as adults. We must redeem the time because we will not have it again.

How are your children spending their time?

PRAYER

Father, thank You for giving us a vision to raise adults rather than entertain children. Grant us wisdom in our selection of activities, so we will choose only those that meet our goal of preparing our children for life. Having fun can be a part of this preparation as we keep our goals in mind. Help us to be creative and to see new options for our children. ❧

FOOD FOR THOUGHT

1. Do the activities that your family pursues fit in with a vision to train children to be thriving adults? Eliminate what is not needed to make room for what is more beneficial.
2. Develop goals for each of your children to help you evaluate opportunities that become available. Say no to the choices that are not consistent with your goals, so you can keep focused on what is best.
3. List skills and character qualities that you want to see in your children when they grow up. List activities that will develop these skills and character qualities. Plan to include some of these in your schedule.

2 8

TALK SOFTLY AND WAIT

By long forbearing is a prince persuaded, and a soft tongue breaketh the bone.

PROVERBS 25:15

✣

*L*earning to make an appropriate appeal to our authorities is a valuable skill that can dramatically alter the course of our life. Unlike the child who stomps his feet and walks away when he encounters the word "no," we can appeal a decision that we feel is not correct. While not always succeeding in changing someone's mind, at the very least a proper appeal will be listened to. At times I realize my husband is not listening to me, and I get frustrated, especially when I am talking about something important.

The problem in many of the cases is that I don't know how to appeal properly. As a woman, I find that my emotions get in the way of what I know I should do. When I am being ignored or misunderstood by Jim, I have to be careful not to react to him. It would be easy to speak harshly and get angry. I have done this, and it never works. In my quest to find a better way, I have discovered that when I wait and am quiet for a minute, Jim will ask me what is wrong. At that time I will be heard if I speak softly and kindly to him. This makes sense to me, but this is not the complete process.

Scripture tells us that "by long forbearing is a prince persuaded." "Long forbearing" means waiting. It might mean waiting a very long time. "A soft tongue breaketh the bone" means that soft words spoken appropriately can accomplish big things. If we speak properly to our husbands and then impose a deadline on his response, we are in for trouble. Men work in their own time frames, and we do well to respect this. When they fail to respond to a proper appeal, it does not mean the answer is no—it just means they haven't responded yet.

It is not easy to wait when the answer is so obvious to you. But if we do not give our husbands space to see it for themselves, we are perceived as being bossy, controlling nags. I am encouraged by Proverbs 25:15 because it gives me a map to get to my destination. It tells me two actions to take. I need to speak softly and to wait. These directions are for me, and I can decide to follow them. It doesn't matter what my husband does; this verse says speaking softly and waiting can persuade a prince. Believe it!

How do you speak to your husband?

PRAYER

Lord, thank You for making Your Word so clear to me in this area. I am motivated by the vision this verse gives me for success. Help me to soften my speech toward my husband. Remind me that waiting is part of the process that develops patience. Please help me keep my emotions in check when I am misunderstood. ❧

FOOD FOR THOUGHT

1. Do you hear the same tone of voice you use toward your husband showing up in the way your children relate to each other? This is too important to ignore.
2. Spend time with women who have sweet speech. Don't be afraid to copy their style as you make a transition into godly, soft-spoken dialogue.
3. Cry out to God for help!

29

HE SENT ME OUT

*Therefore as the church is subject unto Christ, so let the wives
be to their own husbands in every thing.*

EPHESIANS 5:24

❧

When I learned about the glorious role for women that God shows us in
His Word, I gladly embraced coming home from the workforce to be a full-
time wife and mother. I heard the call and was happy to respond. I shelved
any thoughts of future career paths when my children were grown. I was coming home to stay. This would please both God and me, I thought.

For me, however, it wasn't that simple. It took me over five years, from
the time I was writing my first book until after publication of my second book,
to see that God has called me back out of my home in a unique way. As I
fought the concept of juggling family with writing and speaking, my husband could see that God had something planned for us. Jim thinks I am
Superwoman, and I doubted his sanity in the early years of our ministry as I
learned how to balance all of my responsibilities. About the time I thought I
could barely keep up, he would suggest I add one more thing.

I resented this for a long time, and one day we finally ended up in our
pastor's office seeking his opinion on my workload. What he said transformed
my thinking. He asked me what my husband thought. What a wise question. As a wife I am subject to my own husband, and what he thinks reigns
supreme over what anyone else thinks. For better or for worse I have a hus-

band who thinks I can do ten times what I think I am capable of doing. But guess what happened.

Over time I have seen that the organization and management skills God has so graciously provided have helped me do more than I would have attempted without Jim's urging. God has given me a ministry of encouragement to women that I probably would have missed if I had not honored my husband's wishes when circumstances looked foreboding. I have not sidelined my family but instead have provided a rich opportunity for them to learn since their participation in our ministry is vital. I marvel at the way God works out the details when we obey His Word and are subject to our own husbands.

Does your husband want you to do something you are certain you can't do? Is it homeschooling?

PRAYER

Heavenly Father, I appreciate the insight You have given me over the years about my husband's direction. When I have done my best to honor Jim's requests, that has not been wrong. This is not easy for me, and I pray that You would help me to keep following Jim's lead. Thank You for showing me the tremendous fruit that comes from doing just that. ❧

FOOD FOR THOUGHT

1. Are there times when you find your husband asking you to do something that goes entirely in opposition to your own plans? What should you do?
2. If your husband gives you direction, is he confident that you will follow it?
3. The next time your husband asks you to do something you think is unreasonable, cheerfully comply with his request in front of the children. Do this repeatedly and you will see a transformation take place in your family.

30

ARE YOU COMPLETELY DRESSED?

*Put on the whole armor of God, that ye may be able to
stand against the wiles of the devil.*

EPHESIANS 6:11

❧

On a cold December day, six-year-old Joanna had dressed herself in snow-suit, gloves, and hat and had gone outside to play. As I was leaving to go to the store, I looked down at her boots and wondered if her feet were bare as usual. "Joanna, did you put socks on before you put on your boots?" I asked. "Yes, I did," replied my smiling daughter. Hooray! Finally after so many reminders she had taken the initiative herself to get completely dressed before going outside.

How much like her mother she is! Knowing full well how important it is to put on the whole armor of God daily, I have sometimes taken the "easier" route and missed some important things. Armor includes truth, the breastplate of righteousness, the preparation of the Gospel of peace, the shield of faith, the helmet of salvation, and the sword of the Spirit. Just like Joanna, I have sometimes not been protected properly because I have neglected to put on something important.

Truth is faithfulness to do what I know is right. It is my integrity. The breastplate of righteousness is the righteousness of Christ as lived out in my own life. The stability we have from the Gospel gives us a peace to stand in the battle. The shield of faith is our faith in the Lord that is strong enough to stop the arrows that Satan aims at us. The helmet of salvation is spiritual safety, and the sword of the Spirit (the Bible) offers protection.

As I review this list, the hole in my armor is obvious to me. I need to get into God's Word more. Even when I am faithful to read Scripture each day, it never seems like enough. How much damage could Satan do in your life if your mind was saturated with Scripture? The needs of the family and the cares of the day often minimize the time we spend reading the Bible. If we spent more time in God's Word, it is possible that we would not need so much time to spend on the other concerns.

Do you read your Bible daily? For how long?

PRAYER

Father, forgive me for neglecting Your provision for my direction, the Bible. The more I read it, the more I want to spend more time reading it. I miss the answers You have for me when I don't read Your Word. Help me to be more faithful and to expand the amount of time I read the Bible. ❧

FOOD FOR THOUGHT

1. Do you realize that you are in a battle? Armor is mandatory for victory.
2. Do your children have a quiet time when they read their Bibles each day? This habit developed in youth will bless them when their busy adult lives threaten to minimize the time they spend reading the Word of God.
3. Do a study on armor, emphasizing how important it was for the soldier to put on all of his armor before the battle. Make sure your children understand that as Christians we are in a battle and have armor too. Let them tell you how they think they can best remember to put on the whole armor daily.

3 1

I NEED TO TALK

But let none of you suffer as a murderer, or as a thief, or as an
evildoer, or as a busybody in other men's matters.

1 PETER 4:15

I look at people in a positive way. I do not expect them to do wrong or
harm me, but sometimes they do, and I am surprised. There are times when
I find it beneficial to talk through a problem with someone. It is important
that I carefully select the woman to whom I make myself vulnerable.

Women are talkers. We can say too much to the wrong person if we are
not careful. Some women will divulge "secrets" about other people to you, asking that you not repeat the information. Suddenly you find yourself privy to
information about someone else that they probably wouldn't want you to
know. Steer clear from women like this or it will be your downfall. If you
share your struggles with another woman who likes to tell other people what
she knows, likely your difficulties will be broadcast to other people you pre-
fer would not hear about them. We also must be careful that we do not share
what has been told to us in confidence lest we become busybodies ourselves.

It can be very comforting to talk with another woman about our challenges. It is practical and convenient and may yield instant results. I have
experienced this more than once. There is another person, though, who
understands us far better than another woman ever will. The Lord knows you
and all of your difficulties. He made you and allowed your problems to come

into your life for a reason. He knows better than any woman how to help you respond correctly to those struggles.

Women sometimes approach me with their problems and ask me what I think. Many times I have resources that can help them or possibly some insight to head them in the right direction. But my inadequacy at understanding their whole situation is striking. While I can be of some help, I can't know enough to replace what God can show them when they seek answers from Him. When we help other women, our goal should be to point them toward God. We can make suggestions, but we can be wrong. God is never wrong.

Do you seek God to help with your troubles, or are you depending on other people for solutions?

PRAYER

Dear Jesus, I confess that I like to talk to other people. I like dialogue and communicating with flesh and blood that I can see. I forget that no person knows exactly what I need like You do. I can too easily depend on people and forget to seek You. Thank You for answering a prayer so clearly a few weeks ago in a way that nobody else could have done. I only went to You with my question, and You answered immediately. Thank You for showing me what is best. ❧

FOOD FOR THOUGHT

1. Do you have a close friend to share your problems with who will encourage you in the right direction? Make sure she is not one who will share your business with others.
2. Consider taking your problems only to God for a period of time. See how He answers.
3. Reflect back on the times that you received bad counsel from someone. Forgive them now, knowing they didn't understand God's big plan in the matter.

3 2

I Can Ski Again

To every thing there is a season, and a time to every purpose under the heaven.

ECCLESIASTES 3:1

❧

I just finished a refreshing half hour of cross-country skiing with my eight-year-old son Jonathan. His birthday is in October, and we were able to locate a used set of skis, poles, and boots to fit him just in time for winter. This December alone we have seen an accumulation of over fifteen inches of snow on our farm. Ample room to ski and optimal snow conditions have made the first month of winter an excellent time for Jonathan and me to enjoy cross-country skiing together.

Jim and I used to ski before our children were born. We found it impossible to continue with small children and put our gear in the bag. It stayed in the garage unopened for over ten years. I remember sometimes I would look out at the snow and wish I could enjoy the exercise and fresh air that comes with cross-country skiing. But I knew it was too much to get a babysitter and then travel somewhere to ski on trails since we lived in suburban Chicago at the time.

So it goes with homeschooling. There are activities and interests in my life that are no longer convenient to me as a homeschool mother. Oh, I know if I am creative enough I can find the time. But frankly, it just isn't that easy anymore. I accepted the initial sacrifices involved with homeschooling like giving up a weekly Bible study and my craft time. Now what I am having to give up is harder—my time at night to read.

It seems that I get snuggled into bed, finally, and someone crawls up on the bed to talk to me. Other nights I am asleep before my head even hits the pillow. When I had all young children, there was time in the evening to read. Now the older ones need to talk, and there just isn't much time for reading. It won't always be this way, but in this season I have to accept this limitation. Homeschooling mothers have many demands upon their time. So enjoy the children. They grow up too quickly. In a blink of an eye there will once again be opportunity to read, do crafts, and pursue other interests. But for now enjoy your children. What you give up in the process is never worth more than time spent with them.

Do you feel like you have given up much to homeschool? You have, but it was worth it!

PRAYER

Dear God, I appreciate the opportunity You have given me as a homeschool mom to yield my rights. I have been forced to give up many things that I would like to have done so I could follow Your call to our family to homeschool. The character growth for me has been helpful because learning to sacrifice in homeschooling has taught me how to sacrifice in other areas too. ❧

FOOD FOR THOUGHT

1. What have you given up to homeschool? What have you gained?
2. Look for opportunities to take back some of what you have given up, like I did with cross-country skiing.
3. Are there other things that God is asking you to give up? Are you willing?

33

HE BLESSED ME

Therefore I say unto you, What things so ever ye desire,
when ye pray, believe that ye receive them,
and ye shall have them.

MARK 11:24

✻

Some of my prayers go unanswered because of my unbelief. I see life too often from my own limited earthly perspective. I don't really believe in my heart that God can do what seems impossible to me. Ironically, God specializes in doing that very thing.

Recently I began to ask God to bless me on a daily basis patterned after Jabez's calling out to God in 1 Chronicles 4:10. Jabez asked God to bless him, enlarge his coast, keep His hand with Jabez, and keep him from evil so it would not grieve Him. Jabez asked, and Jabez received. Soon after hearing this verse I began in earnest to pray for these things, believing God would do it. The teacher of these truths (Bruce Wilkinson in the book *The Prayer of Jabez*) illustrated God's faithfulness in his own life with many powerful stories. If it worked for him, I reasoned, it should work for me.

Already in a right relationship with the Lord, I found it easy to cry out for greater blessings and ministry, for God's hand to be with me and for me to be kept from evil. I did not doubt He would do all that. And He did! I did not tell God what to do as I prayed. I just asked Him to bless me. Then I began to see wonderful things happen in my life. During the first six weeks I had a dream fulfilled when a corporation asked me to speak at their sales meeting. I was able to share biblical truth in a secular environment. We had a major breakthrough in our marriage in an area of difficulty. Our older children began to demonstrate initiative in ways that blessed our entire family.

We were presented with the opportunity to purchase a car that will facilitate growth in our ministry. While I was praying about that car, I felt the Lord impressing on me that He wanted to bless me. I had never had an experience like this before. We did buy the car, even though it seemed impossible to us at the time. God is blessing in ways I have not noticed before. The difference in my life now is that I believe He will. It doesn't mean everything will be easy. It means when I pray and believe that He will bless according to His perfect will for me, I can count on it.

PRAYER

Father, thank You for teaching me to ask You to bless me. I haven't done this in the past because I thought it was selfish. I did not understand that I needed to ask. You are so generous. Help me to manage the blessings that You give to me. I want to be a good steward of all that I have received. ❧

FOOD FOR THOUGHT

1. Have you ever asked God to bless you on a daily basis? Try it for a couple of weeks, and see if this helps you as you homeschool.
2. We ask God to help us with our children. So why can't we ask Him to bless our children? He will.
3. As you see the fruits of your labor, and as your children are influencing others for Christ, ask God to enlarge their coast (influence). Pray that they would make a difference for Christ in their generation.

34

I Can't Control People

Every wise woman buildeth her house: but the foolish
plucketh it down with her hands.

PROVERBS 14:1

୬୫

My husband asked me to memorize this verse a while ago. I remember thinking at the time that he was attributing every family difficulty to me. You see, I did not really believe he was viewing me as the wise woman, thinking he saw me as the foolish woman. *Great!* I thought. I wasn't too encouraged until the other day.

It was a busy Sunday, and I awoke very tired. I admit I was crabby. It was the first time in a long time, and I was hoping my family would be patient with me. But things didn't go very well because the morning didn't run smoothly, and I had no patience with my children. Since it was that delicate time in my female cycle that Jim knows requires his understanding, I knew I could count on him to help me out.

That's when he told me to take a chill pill. I don't respond very well when my husband talks to me this way under such conditions. He received an icy stare from me. A few more poorly chosen comments on his part took me to a place I did not want to go. I became angry at him for making the situation worse for me. I cried at first, but then the wrong words left my mouth too.

There are times when I do tear down my house. I can't afford to react to my husband or children when they say or do things that can set me off. That always ends up setting the wrong tone in my home and takes a lot of work to repair. This time my family fared pretty well, but I had a severe headache for two days afterward. I had much work to do but was unable to do anything during this time.

We need to learn something from the ducks. Water rolls right off their backs. Other people's words that can offend us need to roll right off our backs. If we pay no heed to them, they won't have any power over us, and we won't end up in the self-destruct mode. Most importantly, it will be counted to us as wisdom since we will be building up our house with our example.

Have you been a wise woman lately?

PRAYER

Heavenly Father, I confess that I have been a foolish woman. I have worked so hard to build up our home, but it doesn't take much for me to tear it down. I don't want to do this anymore. Grow my character to the place where I can let more roll off my back. I particularly need help learning how not to take things so personally. Help me to be the wise woman. ❦

FOOD FOR THOUGHT

1. List ways that a wise woman builds her house. List ways that a foolish woman destroys her house. Check off all that apply to you. Where do you need improvement?
2. Make time to study character for yourself. Your own character development will be reflected in how you run your home.
3. Humble yourself before your husband, and encourage him to tell you what he sees in you that needs improvement. Forget about the delivery—focus on the content of what he is saying. Allow God to use your husband to lead you.

35

MOM IS GLAD AT ME

Abstain from all appearance of evil.

1 THESSALONIANS 5 : 22

❧

At bedtime four-year-old Josiah came down the hall to give me a hug. He asked me if I was "glad" at him. Earlier in the evening a couple of the older children had problem behaviors that did not make me happy. Josiah cautiously was seeking to find out if any of his behavior was troubling me. In his own style he approached me in a positive way, hoping I was glad at him instead of mad at him.

Sometimes I experience sensory overload, and I get a little tense, and my tone of voice changes. I am then more abrupt and impatient. As the stress overtakes me, I am not very relaxed. None of this means that I am angry. The problem is that it may very well look like I am angry. I am passionate about what I believe, and sometimes when I talk, my voice raises in pitch as I get excited. This too can look just like I am angry. The Scripture tells us to abstain from all appearances of evil—all of them. This means that how we look matters.

It is true that it is what is on the inside that counts, but what is showing on the outside needs to be correct. I am conscious of my need to be more calm and peaceful. There are times when I see improvement and then others when I completely fail. My goal is to learn to be sweet and gentle in all the circumstances of life. I don't want there to be anything about me that would lead my children to think I am angry.

This is a pretty tall order, but with God's help you can move in the right direction. Homeschooling provides daily practice in learning to be calm when your natural tendency would be to do the opposite. The whole family benefits when you take these opportunities to learn to stay calm. In light of eternity, most of what ruffles us is of no consequence anyway. Our calm and gentle demeanor sets a warm tone in our home. Children learn how to handle life from us. How we deal with stress shows them what they should do. Our children hear our words and see our actions from early on.

How do your children perceive you?

PRAYER

Dear Lord, I want my example to be a godly one. I want my words, tone of voice, and actions to accurately portray what is on the inside. Please help me to stay calm and gentle within regardless of what is going on. Show me how to express my passion without sounding angry. Please alert me to what needs to change here. ❧

FOOD FOR THOUGHT

1. What do you look like when you are under stress? Does your response to stress give an appearance of evil? How can this be changed?
2. Train your children to stay away from put-downs, sarcasm, and humor at another's expense. Teach them why these all have no place in a godly person's life.
3. What sets you off? People? Events? Once identified, take steps so these triggers do not pull you away from the goal of being sweet and gentle in all circumstances.

3 6

WHAT ABOUT MY SCHEDULE?

In God I will praise his word, in God I have put my trust;
I will not fear what flesh can do unto me.

PSALM 56:4

❦

*I*t had been two years since we set goals for our children. An annual activity developed with my husband, goal-setting provides a target that we can aim for throughout the school year. But urgent needs kept arising after our move to the country, and goal-setting lost its place of priority.

Since we do a lot of independent learning from books in our family, Jim has to make an effort to see what the children are working on. He was busy with a full-time job and farm upkeep and did not really know what the children and I were doing. One time at a meal he made an announcement that rubbed me the wrong way.

"Let's just put the books away and work on farm projects," he directed. I was taken aback since this had not been discussed with me, and we really had no more time to "take off" due to other situations that had arisen during the school year. I reacted to this, and what could have been an opportunity turned into a disaster.

I completely forgot that God is the One in whom I put my trust. I was worried that my husband would mess up my schedule and make it hard for me to get the children back into their books. I wasn't trusting God to work through my husband. Even though Jim had forgotten to check with me before changing our plans, God could have used this in many ways. If I had graciously followed his lead, Jim might have been convicted that he had handled it wrongly. As it was, because I reacted so badly there was little chance that he would see beyond my failure.

Difficult situations are often less important than how we choose to handle them. Whether we worked on farm projects or read our books did not really matter. What mattered was the way Jim and I related to each other in front of the children. Wives need to let God work in the lives of their husbands. While we want to help, we get in God's way by trying to control so many things. It is God in whom we put our trust.

Where do you put your trust?

PRAYER

Father, I know that I should trust You, but I still end up fearing what people can do to me. This is foolish. Flesh can not harm me unless You allow it. Even when everything is out of control and I can't seem to make a difference, it doesn't matter. It isn't up to me—it is up to You. Forgive me for trusting more in my own solutions than in You as the Sovereign One. I am a slow learner lately. ❧

FOOD FOR THOUGHT

1. Does your husband understand your routine and the priorities you have for your school? It helps if you can set this up together.
2. Visualize how you would have handled the situation at our meal table differently. Remember this the next time your husband does something similar.
3. Can God really be trusted to work everything out when it looks hopeless? Doesn't He need our help? (Yes, He can; and no, He doesn't.)

37

I'm Working on It

Nevertheless let every one of you in particular so love his wife even as himself; and the wife see that she reverence her husband.

EPHESIANS 5:33

⁓

*A*t two years old Julianne had quite a vocabulary. Every day she would speak a new word we had not heard before. One day the children were getting ready to play in a little pool in our yard. Julianne was excited to put on her "swimming soup," as she put it. Nobody thought this to be out of the ordinary for her since she was still in the process of developing her language.

Why, then, am I so hard on myself when I don't get the biblical principle of reverencing my husband exactly right? I had no understanding of this concept until midlife. Since this very important behavior for a wife is relatively new to me, I am still in the process of learning to apply it in my marriage. Just as Julianne will continue to improve in her understanding and use of the English language, so will I grow, Lord willing, in respecting my husband.

As we mature in our Christian walk, we will see more godly behavior develop in our lives. The process can be painful as we experience the consequences of mistakes that we make as we are learning. But the more we practice right behaviors, the closer these come to being good habits. As in anything, you can't expect to start with perfection. You have to get started and keep making improvements along the way. All of my children said some pretty funny words when they first began to talk. They grew through this awkward first stage and went on to become clear communicators. I did not expect as much from them at the beginning as I do now.

Giving your husband respect as the leader of your family may not come easy to you if you are not familiar with living this out daily. It takes time to change old habits. Give yourself some room to grow in this area, and watch for progress. As you reverence your husband, you give God the respect He deserves. Husbands don't always act as they should, but we are to reverence them because of their position, not because of the way they act. This sounds as difficult as learning to talk.

Do your children talk? How much better are they now than when they first started? See, with God's help, you can learn to respect your husband too!

PRAYER

Dear God, it is easier for me to give my children room to grow than it is to be patient with my own growth. Help me to stop looking for finished products and to learn to love the progress. Give me a clearer picture of what I should look like when I am reverencing Jim. Please hurry—I don't think I understand this too well. ❧

FOOD FOR THOUGHT

1. Do your children respect you? Is that a reflection on the respect that you show your husband?
2. This verse shows us what God requires of both husbands and wives that does not come naturally. Are you making it easy for your husband to love you? What can you do to help yourself reverence your husband? Memorize Ephesians 5:33.
3. Praise God for specifically showing us in His Word what He wants us to do.

38

No Longer the Schoolmaster

But after that faith is come, we are no longer under a schoolmaster.

GALATIANS 3:25

❧

I am longing for the day when my children walk in truth because they have made it their own in their hearts. They will do what is right because it is right and they want to please God. They will act voluntarily rather than acting in fear of Dad or Mom. They will become adults who are responsible to God for who they are and what they do. I have seen some evidence of this already in my older children.

The Greek word translated "schoolmaster" means child-discipliner or child-trainer. That is who we are as homeschool moms. We are the trainers who are pointing our children to Christ. Our ultimate goal is for them to seek to glorify Christ in their own lives, motivated by an internal desire to do what's right. The challenge we have is that this process takes time—a long time. Our children need our loving guidance and persevering patience to grow. The years where they are doing right things only because we told them to last quite a while. We hope for the day they wake up one morning and show us the fruit we have been patiently seeking over the years. After almost fifteen years of parenting, this very blessing was bestowed upon me.

During a busy six weeks this spring my two oldest daughters assumed a greater share of the responsibilities in the home than usual. On the second day of a three-day homeschool convention, Jamie, age fourteen, completely surprised me. On that day she was responsible for baby-sitting five of our children, ages three to ten. This is a task for me, and when the older girls are not home, I'm sure I would not take on any "extra" projects.

When I returned in the evening, Jamie showed me matching jumpers she had made for our two youngest daughters. I was ecstatic! I had taught her to sew years ago, but she didn't seem too interested. The next night I came home and found she had made herself a dress with a matching jacket. It took time, but Jamie has now taken this sewing ability and made it her own. She sews because she wants to, not because I am telling her she should. This same process takes shape in young men and young women as the Bible truths we teach them become their own.

Are you waiting for fruit? Don't give up—it will come!

PRAYER

Dear Jesus, thank You for showing me the wisdom of teaching my children and then encouraging them. By not forcing them to do everything, I have given You a chance to work in their hearts and make the truth their own. Please help me to take more opportunities to share biblical truth with them throughout the events of each day. Teaching them skills seems to come more naturally than teaching them character. Help me to make character training a habit. ❧

FOOD FOR THOUGHT

1. Pick up a copy of *Proverbs for Parenting* by Barbara Decker, arranged topically to help you instruct your children in biblical truth.
2. Fruit matures slowly. List all of the blossoms you have seen in your children so far as an encouragement.
3. Learn to do what is right (train your children in biblical truth) without immediate gratification (fruit). Your character is growing again!

39

CALL ON GOD

Call unto me, and I will answer thee, and show thee great and mighty things, which thou knowest not.

JEREMIAH 33:3

I have been learning to go to God right away and tell Him my difficulties. It is my nature to try and resolve problems myself, which leaves God completely out of the process. By taking things to God in prayer first, I have found much needed direction that I could not have found on my own.

About a week ago I had taken one of our business checks out of a big binder and put it in my purse. We were making a purchase that we thought would be paid for by our business. But we decided to write a personal check instead. I usually return unused business checks to the binder right away. In the busy holiday season I had forgotten.

When I opened the binder to pay some business bills, I was dismayed to find the check missing. It was a couple of days after returning to our full school schedule after the holidays, and my head was crammed full of details. I could barely remember the last time I saw the check, let alone where I had put it.

I prayed, acknowledging that God knew all about the check and where it was. I asked for direction regarding what to do. It was night, and I was already in bed. Jim came to bed later, and we began to discuss the missing check. He said it wasn't like me to lose a check and that it must be somewhere in our home. I had checked my purse thoroughly a couple of times and could not think of anywhere else to look. Then Jim asked if I'd looked in my coat pocket. That was it! I went downstairs, checked my coat, and found the missing check.

God worked through my husband to show me what I needed to know. He could have used my children for the same purpose. How much easier the situation is when we go to God first and ask for His help. Sometimes God allows problems that we won't be able to solve on our own. It should have been easy for me to remember where I put the check, but I could not. God's power is clearly displayed each time we turn our troubles over to Him. He works things out so differently from what we could have seen in our own minds. It is peaceful to call out to God, knowing that He has promised to answer and to show us what we do not know.

Have you called on God for help recently?

PRAYER

Heavenly Father, forgive me for forgetting to take my problems to You first. You are faithful to answer when I call, but I must make the call. I am encouraged by remembering how well it goes for me when I seek You. When other people have no answers, You always do. Help me to keep this in mind at all times. ❧

FOOD FOR THOUGHT

1. Does God hear from you very often when you are in need of answers? Make prayer to Him the first call that you make.
2. Think about the times God has provided answers that you could not have thought of on your own. Let this encourage you to rest in His power and not your own.
3. God knows more about homeschooling than anyone. Just ask Him!

4 0

HORMONALLY HARASSED

Our soul waiteth for the LORD: he is our help and our shield.
For our heart shall rejoice in him, because we have
trusted in his holy name.

PSALM 33:20-21

*U*pon entering our favorite Mexican restaurant for lunch, I pulled one of our business cards out of my purse to drop in the bowl so they would send us a coupon for a free dinner. I was alone. I had gone out for a mental health day—the term I use for a much needed teacher's institute day. As I looked down at the business card I read the logo: "With God All Things Are Possible." I noticed this in a special way.

I felt sure that my situation was impossible, and I wondered how I would get through it. Basically burned out and hormonally harassed, I was enduring my fifth miscarriage in eighteen months. This mental health day was part of our plan to keep me from completely breaking down. That doesn't sound very conducive to homeschooling, does it? It wasn't. I just had to take a break.

My soul was troubled. I wanted to give up. Beyond the *why* stage, I was asking God *how* questions. How can I homeschool a large family when my hormones are fluctuating so far and fast that I resemble a creature from the deep on some days? How can I teach character to my children when my behavior is so erratic? How will my daughters see children as a blessing when they keep seeing me suffer? The *how* questions kept coming.

The answers to the *how* questions never specifically came. But my soul did recover, and I did rejoice in the Lord again. I have learned to trust God in the area of children because unless I claim His promises, I can't understand my circumstances. I had to do some waiting, but in time I felt peace. In the past two days I have learned that I am pregnant again. I am tired and starting to feel a little poorly. New *how* questions are arising, like: How can I finish this devotional now? I will do it through the grace of God, and my soul is not troubled because I put my trust in Him for the outcome of this pregnancy.

Is your soul troubled? Don't rush things. Give God a chance to be your help.

PRAYER

Dear Lord, thank You for giving me the opportunity to trust You once again for the blessing of a child. You know my fears, and I trust You to be with me throughout this pregnancy. No matter what the outcome, I know that You are there and will be my help. I trust You. ❧

FOOD FOR THOUGHT

1. Do you need a break? Take one. If a day out by yourself will recharge you, take one as often as needed. Paying a baby-sitter is a wise investment if that is what you need to do.
2. Can you rejoice in God in the midst of trials? Are you trusting in His name? If not, where do you put your trust? Does that work?
3. Remember that God loves you. No matter what you are going through, God knows and in some way will use it for good in your life if you let Him. The trial itself won't necessarily be good, but what comes from the trial can be priceless.

41

GO BACK TO BED

The fear of the LORD is the instruction of wisdom;
and before honour is humility.

PROVERBS 15:33

*J*immy was supposed to be in bed, but he wasn't. Since he was nine years old, I saw no reason for him to be getting up after he was told to be in bed. Bedtime is not the strongest part of the day for me. Jim works overnight as a fire-fighter every third day; so I am alone in the evening, putting the children to bed by myself. After spending twelve or more hours together, bedtime signi-fies to me that my "kid day" is over. I use this term to let my children know that I have nothing left for them on that particular day.

I get impatient when the children (especially the older ones) get up after being sent to bed. This night was no exception. I impulsively accused Jimmy of playing in the bathroom instead of obeying. Actually, he was obey-ing by filling the humidifier as he had been instructed. He remembered in bed that he had forgotten and had gotten up to finish the task. Boy, did I blow it!

The greatest issue here was not that I became impatient. It was not that I jumped to conclusions and wrongly accused my child. These are important matters, but the greatest issue was how I dealt with the mistake that I had made. Once I realized what had happened, I humbled myself to Jimmy and said I was sorry. No excuses needed to be made about being tired at the end of the day or anything else. I simply needed to admit my error and make it right.

There are endless opportunities in a homeschool day for us to make bad choices in regard to our children. If they know that we are open to their coming to us with their concerns, we can learn a lot from their observations. Humility takes work; pride comes naturally. If we are too proud to admit our mistakes, we lose a lot of teaching potential. The details of each incident are in many cases soon forgotten. But how we choose to respond to them will be remembered by our families. Make it a goal to be humble to your children. They can see what is wrong anyway, even if you don't admit it. It is far better to teach humility in the process than to model pride.

Is God teaching you to be humble? He is working on me!

PRAYER

Lord, thank You for forcing me to learn to be humble in the context of homeschooling. I can think of no better accountability relationship than this one. My family needs to feel open to share their concerns with me. I confess that I have not made it easy for them. Help me to be open to the correction You can provide for me through my family. Let our home be a place where we all learn to build each other up by the way we address such problems. ✌

FOOD FOR THOUGHT

1. Have you ever thought of allowing your children to hold you accountable for your behavior? Done respectfully by older children, this can deepen your relationship with them.
2. Do you jump to conclusions before finding out the facts with your children? Be careful. Learn to be the detective, not the uniformed police officer.
3. Do a character study for yourself on humility. Allow God to develop this in you.

4 2

I Am Running Away

And I said, Oh that I had wings like a dove!
For then would I fly away, and be at rest.

PSALM 55:6

⊷

I don't remember thinking much about running away as a child. But as an adult this thought recurs. When I struggle with relationships in my family, sometimes I wish I could disappear for a while. If Jim and I are communicating poorly, the hurt can go so deep that I just want to run. The fight or flight instinct kicks in, and I have to make an effort to make the right decision. Relationship pressures in the homeschool family are real and have real consequences. We must deal with conflicts or face those consequences.

Homeschool families are not immune from rebellious children. As we learn to raise our children for Christ, the baggage in our own lives produces less than desirable results at times. The oldest child in the family is more prone to rebellion for many reasons, although any of your children can rebel at any time. I have watched a number of women work through the painful experience of losing one of their children to rebellion. Some of the children repent, and relationships are healed. For others it is not so easy.

Our closest relationships are the ones that can cause us the deepest pain. Because we spend so much time together as a family, the potential for wounding is very real. If we learn to work through our relational difficulties, we are going to be stronger. When we struggle and cannot seem to get it right, the pain is searing. All of a sudden you may feel like you are done. Finished. You can't take another minute. You want to run. You want to flee. You think that running from the problems will bring you peace. You cease to care about resolving anything. You just want it to be over.

God is the only one who brings you peace. He can do this even in the middle of tremendous relationship problems. Running from them only makes things worse, even though it seems like making a quick exit would give you the rest you desire. But it won't hurt to take a break in the middle of demanding trials. Do something you enjoy for a day without worrying about other responsibilities. Spend more time in the Psalms when you are in need of comfort. Draw closer to God, and He will help you sort out your relationships. Be open to what may need to change in your own life as well as in the lives of others in the family.

Relationships take work. Are you working hard?

PRAYER

Father, how foolish I feel when, knowing I need to work through relationship problems, I still get that urge to run from time to time. Help me to remember that this solves nothing and is only a temporary break. Show me how to be peaceful amidst the storms. Carry me when I can't seem to manage. ❧

FOOD FOR THOUGHT

1. Get a video or audio cassette of "Changing the Heart of a Rebel" from Dr. S. M. Davis (1-800-500-8853).
2. Do you avoid conflict? Learn to face problems and work through them. Problems that are ignored are still problems and will surface again later.
3. Have you run away from your relationships? Come back and seek God's best for resolution.

4 3

GOD IS GOOD

One generation shall praise thy works to another,
and shall declare thy mighty acts.

PSALM 145:4

❧

I have noticed that I share my struggles and concerns with my children openly but then forget to point out God's goodness in helping me. It is incomplete training on my part as a mother to tell my children about problems without relating to them how God deals with them in my life. God's presence every day is real, and I need to show this to my children in specific ways.

Last year right after a miscarriage I suffered another loss. Our eleven-month-old collie, Callie, got into some poison and became very sick. The toxin is so poisonous to collies in particular that just getting it on her teeth was enough to kill her. Suddenly my Lassie look-alike, which we intended to breed, did not look like she would make it to her first birthday. Just hours after chewing on a tube of goat wormer she was foaming at the mouth and having seizures.

We followed the veterinarian's advice and made her vomit, but the toxin had already entered her system. A specialist was called, and it was determined that although there was a good possibility Callie would recover with no permanent damage, there were no guarantees. The cost to medicate her and treat her at the vet's would be a minimum of 700 or 800 dollars. The cost could easily run higher. Even if we had the money, we could not justify committing to something like this for an animal when we had seven children to care for.

Heavy of heart, we signed the paper authorizing the vet to put her to sleep. It all seemed so unfair. Our first dog had been a seventy-five-pound nightmare that lived with us for eleven years. Now we had a great dog, and she only lasted eleven months. My ability to cope with loss was at an all-time low. In a few days we seemed to be accepting what had happened, but our other collie, Brenna, was not eating and moped around. I saw that we would need to replace Callie with a puppy the next spring.

Thinking that God would help us deal with our loss, it had briefly occurred to me along the way that maybe God would prevent the loss. Our vet was troubled to have to put such a good dog to sleep when there was a good prognosis for recovery. We felt the same way. I passed off the thought that she would treat and heal Callie without charge because vets could not stay in practice very long if they rescued many animals like our collie. About a week before Christmas I got a vague call from our vet requesting that Jim and I stop by her office. We went and were greeted by Callie! Our vet had cared for her for a full two weeks before Callie even moved. Over the next month she gradually regained her strength and now is fully recovered. Only God could move the heart of our vet to do us such a favor. She had never done anything like this before.

Have you pointed out God's goodness to your children lately?

PRAYER

Dear Lord, thank You, thank You, thank You. ❧

FOOD FOR THOUGHT

1. Look for God's goodness in each day.
2. Pray that God will work miracles.
3. Believe that God will answer your prayers.

44

It's Not Up to Me

Being confident of this very thing, that he which hath begun a good work in you will perform it until the day of Jesus Christ.

PHILIPPIANS 1:6

Before lunch I headed up to my bedroom to shed a few tears. I had given our morning of homeschooling everything I had, but it was obvious that I was no match for the needs of the day. The two- and four-year-olds were aggravating each other. The work of my high schooler hadn't been reviewed lately. And the fourth grader was still having trouble sitting down and staying focused on his work. Then there were the two new readers who still needed a lot of my attention.

When I am rested, healthy, and vibrant, I can usually handle all of this. Today this was not the case. I was tired and could not keep up with the demands made of me. I was out of energy. This has happened before. Regardless of what brings me to this point, it blesses my children.

Yes, I said they are blessed. The less I can do, the more they must do. They are forced to take more initiative when I am in a weakened state. This happens because we have laid a foundation of responsibility and work in our home. There can be limited progress in the children in these areas until I am down for some reason, and then they step in and take up the slack. This is good! While I feel I am somehow letting them down, I am actually blessing them with the chance to make a difference in our family life.

Children need to try out what they have been taught. If Mom is always doing it for them, they are handicapped learners. As I am faithful to teach them, God is faithful to help them apply what they are learning. It's not up to me to be sure every training need of every child in our home is met all of the time. I could never do the job, but God can. Character strengths and weaknesses are out in the open, and we can praise or correct them. Whether or not the children embrace our work ethic shows. God began a good work in our children, and He will perform it until the day of Christ. As each child comes to know Jesus as his or her personal Savior, this promise becomes his or her own.

Are you trying to do it all? Stop it! You are just wearing yourself out.

PRAYER

God, thank You for showing me Your role in homeschooling. I feel guilty when I can't keep up with everything because I keep thinking everything is up to me. I know that You will finish what I am beginning with my children, and I don't need to put so much pressure on myself. Thank You for giving me a new perspective on the times when I must rest, seeing them as opportunities for my children to learn to take more responsibility. ❧

FOOD FOR THOUGHT

1. Do you encourage your children to do as much as possible on their own at an early age? Bless them by allowing them to learn to be responsible.
2. Are you training your children to run the house? This is the time for them to learn.
3. Are you unsure of your ability to homeschool? Don't worry—God will help you when you ask.

45

God Sets the Priorities

Except the LORD build the house, they labour in vain that build it:
except the LORD keep the city, the watchman waketh but in vain.

PSALM 127:1

*H*ave you ever eaten too much cookie dough? You know that sick feeling in your stomach that makes you think you are going to throw up, but you don't. I feel that way about homeschooling in February—every year. It is a restless time. We are tired of schoolbooks, but it isn't warm enough yet for outdoor work and play. This is similar to the feeling at the end of the summer when the children are restless because of too much free time. The antidote is the same.

We need balance. Too much school or too much free time both produce that same restlessness. As homeschool moms we have the flexibility to change our schedules. Summer can be a time of casually reviewing math facts, reading stories aloud, and getting to those crafts we never seem to have time for during the other months. Winter can be a perfect opportunity for a day at Grandma's, a trip to a museum, or an overnight "vacation" for the family at a hotel—just for fun.

Our priorities each day determine the balance in our lives. If we are following agendas and schedules that we have set ourselves, we are likely to be out of balance. God's plans for our days are often different than our plans. If we seek Him first and follow Him, I wonder, will balance return? If I stopped worrying about finishing the books and let us all rest for a few days in February, I wonder if the restlessness would be gone. If I were more faithful to have scheduled time in the summer, would that bring back balance? Only the Lord can show me on a daily basis what is truly important. I have to take the initiative to ask Him.

We need to have plans and routines that are adaptable. When planning the school year, factor in a couple of extra weeks because likely by the end you will have used them. School in our homes is not like the traditional school that most of us attended. It is dynamic and changing. We remember the bell ringing every single day at exactly the same times, but our children will have no such memories. They shouldn't. Life doesn't run by a series of bells. Real life is dynamic and changing; so our flexible homeschooling routines do more to prepare them for real life.

Are you too rigid in your planning? Let God make some adjustments.

PRAYER

Dear Lord, I am so glad that You have shown me how to relax in my scheduling. I have seen You work in the flexibility of each day. Help me to stay in balance. I want to be sensitive to the needs of my children. Show me how to help them learn to be flexible and to allow Your changes to their plans to bless them. ❧

FOOD FOR THOUGHT

1. What throws your homeschool out of balance? How can you change that?
2. Do you plan on having interruptions to your schedule? They will happen.
3. Consider scheduling impromptu days off to work on something else when the restlessness comes.

4 6

A GOOD EXAMPLE

Let no man despise thy youth; but be thou an example of the believers,
in word, in conversation, in charity, in spirit, in faith, in purity.

1 TIMOTHY 4:12

❧

*H*omeschooling offers the right set of circumstances to provide our children with a good example of godly character. We can demonstrate proper ways of relating to other people even when they are being difficult. We can teach our children the value of work and the blessings of a task completed. We can offer hope to them in times of trouble by the faith we have during our own challenges. We can be meek and gentle especially during times of pressure. We can be sweet every day.

Do these statements make you nervous? That's the effect they have on me. I don't always feel like being a good example all day every day. My tongue doesn't always say kind words. My behavior is sometimes exactly the same thing I am trying to correct in my children. I am not always loving, I am sometimes doubtful about God's promises, and I am not sweet all of the time.

We will never be perfect, but we can decide to value the influence we have on our children. We are still young, as mothers, but we can be wise and can determine to be a good example of a godly woman to our children and others. I don't have to wait until I am seventy years old to have a good testimony. I can have spiritual maturity sooner if I allow the magnifying glass that God is putting over me in front of my children to do its work.

Character flaws in the homeschooling mom are part of the curriculum. If we humble ourselves and face our deficiencies as they are made known to us, we give God the freedom to accelerate our learning. I want my children to learn to do the same thing. What an opportunity to model openness for growth in the Christian life to our children, who see us for what we are all day long. How encouraging it will be for them to watch us gain victory in specific areas as we grow in Christ. The testimony of a godly mother is powerful.

How is your testimony doing today?

PRAYER

Heavenly Father, I confess that I don't take my example to my children seriously enough. My influence in their lives is greater than I realize. I pray that it would be an influence for good and not bad. Even when they see my flaws, help me to be humble and to model good character during my mistakes. I know I can't be perfect, but I want to be the best I can be. Help me to do better than I am now, for their sake and for Your glory. ❧

FOOD FOR THOUGHT

1. Do you realize that no matter how you feel or what you are thinking, you still should be a good testimony to your children? Evaluate how you are doing.
2. Do you need to go to your husband or children and ask forgiveness for being a bad example? Humility in the mother sets the stage for character growth in the rest of the family.
3. Pray for God to help you to be a godly woman. It isn't easy to be a godly woman, but it's the best thing you could do.

47

SHE DIDN'T DO IT

*Counsel in the heart of man is like deep water; but a man
of understanding will draw it out.*

PROVERBS 20:5

❧

I have a teenaged daughter who doesn't care much for one of her academic subjects. She excels in just about everything except math. It's not that she doesn't understand it as much as the fact that she hates it. I understand this. Math was something I endured in school. Eventually I had a business calculus class in college that I got an A in, even though I could not tell you anything about calculus now. In order to graduate, I had to persevere in this area I disliked.

During a challenging school year when my health was compromised by several miscarriages, I found that I could not keep up with all of my children's schoolwork. I decided to rely on my oldest child to keep current in the work I had laid out for her. Several times just as I was about to review her work, something came up that postponed my time with her.

Finally after Christmas we sat down to go over her papers. As I wrote out her next math lessons in her assignment notebook, she made no mention of what I was about to discover. Her math notebook reflected completed lessons up through the beginning of October, no farther. How could she be so far behind?

This wasn't about math. It was about diligence to do what is requested of us even when it is difficult or brings us displeasure. She graciously took over all of our meal preparations during the times I needed rest. She enjoyed this but failed to follow through on something she did not enjoy—math. After the discovery of the unfinished lessons, she worked hard and caught up before the end of the school year.

I'm glad I talked with her about the need to do her work regardless of whether she likes it. If I had ranted on about math, I would not have been able to draw out the deeper character issue of diligence. I know better now how to encourage her and also that I should follow up more closely with her.

Do you look below the surface problems to get at the root issues?

PRAYER

Jesus, You are such a good example to me of helping others to see the needs in their lives. You spoke to the heart of the matter without condemning people, so they would listen. Help me to be sensitive to the deeper issues in the lives of my children. Let me see through the surface right to the heart where the changes take place. ❧

FOOD FOR THOUGHT

1. Do you view the failures of your children as training opportunities or frustrations? Your attitude will affect how well you deal with the problems.
2. Do your children only do their work because they know you will check it? Work toward a healthy attitude that finishes work because it is the right thing to do.
3. Do you complain about the work that you do not enjoy? Make an effort to be more positive about the unpleasant tasks you have to do. Your positive attitude will be contagious.

48

WHAT DOES HE THINK OF ME?

The sacrifices of God are a broken spirit: a broken and a contrite heart, O God, thou wilt not despise.

PSALM 51:17

I behaved badly. A combination of stress, hormones, and fear set the stage for behavior in me that resembled a woman losing her mind. I was not myself. I said and did things that I wanted to take back. Jim suffered the most. Nothing he did or said helped me. In fact, it just made it worse.

Days later when I was myself again, a profound remorse came over me. Of course I regretted the mean things I had said. But would Jim hold them against me? He always forgives me, but I still felt like this time I had blown it for the rest of my life. I understand how destructive words can be. Friendships dissolve over just a few poorly chosen comments. How could a marriage withstand the lengthy verbal onslaught Jim had received not just this time but in times past too?

My spirit was broken. Even though there were some pressures behind my wrong behavior, I doubted that I would be understood. How does a man understand the erratic behavior of his burned-out, newly pregnant, afraid-of-another-miscarriage, forty-one-year-old wife? After realizing that Jim was dealing with me the best way he knew how, I wondered what God thought of me.

Was I a hopeless case? Even after studying God's truth during that trying time, I did not apply it. Did God really forgive me for my angry outburst, my questioning God's timing in allowing me to conceive again so soon when I'd only end up miscarrying anyway? The answer lies in verse 17 of Psalm 51.

How we respond to our sin determines how God views us in relation to that sin. Pride keeps us from admitting that what we are doing is wrong. When pride is in control, we can successfully convince ourselves that we have done nothing wrong and then fail to repent and be forgiven. Pride is really another sin, and we are blocking fellowship with God when we embrace this wrong. Humility allows us to admit our guilt and to be restored with people and with God. God looks favorably on a humble heart. Humility is best learned the hard way. A broken heart is able to be used by God; a prideful heart is useless. We get to the place where our heart is broken only through trials and pain. But once we are there, God will not despise us.

Have you done something wrong in a big way? Have you dealt with it properly yet?

PRAYER

Dear Jesus, help me to deal with difficult circumstances with gentleness and peace. My anger never works Your righteousness, and it just ends up disturbing my own soul. It destroys relationships. Thank You for the blessing of a broken heart. I feel free to come to You to ask forgiveness for my failures. I know that You do not reject me for them as people might. Help me to show more humility to my family when I do wrong. ❧

FOOD FOR THOUGHT

1. Does stress overcome you? Take up walking thirty minutes a day to help you relax. It has many other benefits too.
2. Confess your sins regularly. Keep a short list.
3. Forgive others who treat you badly.

4 9

LEARNING IS ALL THE TIME

*And these words, which I command thee this day, shall be in
thine heart: And thou shalt teach them diligently unto
thy children, and shalt talk of them when thou sittest
in thine house, and when thou walkest by the way, and
when thou liest down, and when thou risest up.*

DEUTERONOMY 6:6-7

The longer I homeschool, the less I feel constrained by textbooks and school
schedules. All of life is really our curriculum. Every day holds learning opportunities if we look for them. Learning does not only take place at scheduled
times and places. Some of our most productive learning experiences have
nothing to do with our scheduled "book school."

One of the goals we had in moving to our ten-acre farm was to provide
our children with a varied selection of extraordinary opportunities to learn.
This includes having a collection of animals that resembles a petting zoo.
Recently our pony gave birth to a filly (that's farm talk for girl pony). Often
these births take place in the middle of the night. Ours was born in the
evening. Jim discovered the event as he went to the barn to finish chores
after supper. We dropped everything to run out and observe the new pony.
Unscheduled though it was, it was a superior learning experience.

Jim and the children had watched a video that taught them how to
desensitize the new pony so she would be gentle and easier to train to ride.

Everyone participated in this process by either helping or watching. While our younger children watched, four-year-old Josiah had a question. "Where did the colt come from?" he asked. It made me realize how all the different ages in our family would have a different level of understanding regarding our new pony.

I am grateful that we have so many ways to train our children. We are not limited by desks and clocks, although we do have some of each in our home. We can take a field trip at any time. We can choose to investigate the areas that we find interesting. We can stretch the minds of our children by providing them with rich learning experiences.

Are you chained to your textbooks? Try something new.

PRAYER

Father, thank You for showing me that learning takes place all of the time. Spiritual truths can be taught all day long in the context of daily living. Help me to be more creative as I seek ways to stimulate the thinking of my children. Bless them with a never-ending desire to learn. ❧

FOOD FOR THOUGHT

1. What percentage of your teaching time relates to textbooks? Teach your children how to learn from life. Ask questions that stimulate discussion between family members. Encourage children to talk about what they are interested in, so that others may learn by listening to them. This refines listening skills at the same time.
2. Is teaching our children a matter of our standing up and giving them information, or is it about teaching them how to learn?
3. Think about your own education. What could have been different to take the boredom out of school? Is your school interesting? What radical changes could you make to stimulate your children? Are there other families you could observe in order to get some ideas?

50

SHE'S AT THE END OF HER NOODLE

And not only so, but we glory in tribulations also:
knowing that tribulation worketh patience.

ROMANS 5:3

One day my husband warned the children, "Mom is at the end of her noodle." It sounded silly, but he was right. I had had enough! "Leave me alone," summed up all I wanted to say at that moment. How did it get to that point? Why couldn't I handle all of the demands being made of me just then?

Imagine one spaghetti noodle that symbolizes patience. My children were taking bites off my noodle (my patience) each time they disobeyed and bickered with each other. Jim took a bite with his insensitivity and each unkind word he spoke to me. I don't usually get impatient right away. But as bites off the noodle continue until the noodle is gone, I tend to react in some negative way. Even one sentence spoken sharply does damage.

I cannot afford to reach the end of my noodle. I need to learn to allow God to stretch the noodle out to make it longer during times of trial so that I have enough patience. My flesh reacts to my husband and children because I don't allow the Holy Spirit to guide me as they bite off the noodle. The only true teacher of patience is trial. Expect some poor results at the beginning of your training. Homeschooling is a trial in terms of constant demands on the mother. When you start homeschooling, it is obvious that you don't have enough patience, because you haven't experienced enough of the trial to develop the much desired patience.

Over time if you allow the homeschooling lifestyle to grow you in the direction God desires, you will see that you have greater patience. You are not a failure if you start out impatient. You are successful if there is steady progress in the direction of greater patience. It has taken a long time, but I now see how patience has come only through the trials. So many things that used to bother me, I do not even notice now. As I identify certain situations that still make me impatient, I have noticed that often a trial will come that forces me to address this area. This is good. I want to be the most patient homeschool mom possible for my children.

How much patience do you have today? It's okay. God wants you to have more.

PRAYER

Heavenly Father, thank You for providing tribulation in my life to teach me patience. I don't like the tribulation itself, but I can see it is worth it for the fruit of patience it produces. Please help me to teach my children how to develop patience through their trials. Thank You that I am spending more time at peace than in frustration. What a surprise it has been to see how much homeschooling is teaching me. ❧

FOOD FOR THOUGHT

1. Do you know anyone patient enough to take on homeschooling? Neither do I. Patience is developed on the job.
2. What trial is troubling you right now? How can this trial help you become more patient?
3. Telling children "no" in answer to their requests can be frustrating for them. This is not bad. Teach them how to transform frustration into peace as they understand how God allows our circumstances to bring growth in our lives.

5 1

DISCOURAGED BY THE FOOLISH

He that walketh with wise men shall be wise: but
a companion of fools shall be destroyed.

PROVERBS 13:20

When our oldest, Jamie, was three years old, we lived in suburban Chicago. It was as natural as breathing to send your child to preschool at age three. Knowing nothing of homeschooling, we sent her for one semester to a Bible church preschool. The teachers were nice, and it seemed like the right thing to do. Up until that time Jamie was very creative and liked to draw. It seemed logical that she would do well at preschool. Instead the opposite happened.

During a coloring activity some of the children ridiculed Jamie and told her she didn't know how to color. Jamie stopped coloring at home. After finding out what had happened, we encouraged her to color again. We told her the other children were wrong. It didn't help. She did not color again for over a year. At age fifteen she still remembers the incident clearly. If this one negative situation impacted my three-year-old in this way, what would have happened if we had left her in the preschool? She wasn't surrounded by teachers (wise) but rather by a room full of three-year-olds (fools). It was not good for her. It would be no better now as a teen to be surrounded by fools.

Our children need to be in the companionship of wise people. Wisdom is the knowledge of what is true or right coupled with good judgment. It means making the same choice that God would make. Who among us is wise?

Anyone can be a fool. It is easy. Adults can be fools just as children can be fools. Wise people are truth-seekers. They want to understand God's Word and apply it to their lives. They seek counsel from wise people when they are unsure. We are wise to seek the companionship of the wise for ourselves and for our children. Foolish friends not only bring harm but can destroy you.

Seeking God's best for our families makes sense. In the process we will make mistakes. We didn't know that preschool would be such a negative experience for Jamie. We learned our lesson and made corrections. Selecting activities and friendships that are wise can be challenging. But people who seem very wise can turn out to be fools. We can only do our best to honor God in our friendships and then make changes when we find out we have made a mistake. We are not better than other people, but we want to be sure that the people we spend our time with are wise.

Would people who know you say you are wise or foolish?

PRAYER

Dear Jesus, help me to be one of the wise ones. Show me Your truth, and help me as I apply it. Grant me discernment to know which activities and friendships are best for myself and for my family. I want to please You. ✥

FOOD FOR THOUGHT

1. Do your children play unsupervised with other children? What are they learning?
2. How do you decide if activities or friendships are appropriate? Give more consideration to these in light of what the Bible says about wisdom.
3. Memorize Proverbs 13:20.

52

WE MADE IT TO THE PARADE

The father of the righteous shall greatly rejoice: and he that begetteth
a wise child shall have joy of him. Thy father and
thy mother shall be glad, and she that bare thee shall rejoice.

PROVERBS 23:24-25

❧

I really did not want to go to the parade. Our small town has an annual
town fest that includes a parade. It is small, but I was tired from a church
activity the night before. Jim was at work, and I had no plans to take the
children. I let them sleep in as I worked on this devotional. One hour before
the parade was to begin, somebody mentioned they wanted to go. It was
then that I got an idea.

I told them that if they could all get up on their own, feed themselves, get
the barn chores done (including milking the goats), *and* get ready to go by
themselves, I would take them. I went back to my work doubting they could
do this. After all, on Sunday morning when we get up on time with a plan to
get ready for church, we still have trouble sometimes, even when I am helping. A few minutes passed, and I noticed that more people were stirring in the
house. They seemed pretty organized, and it was pretty calm. I kept on
working at the computer, leaving them completely to themselves. Finally I
had to go upstairs and change into "going to town" clothes. In forty-five
minutes they were all ready to go.

I'm glad I took them to the parade. It was a sunny day, and they had fun. I sat on a chair that one of my sons had thoughtfully put in the van. Six-year-old Joanna brought her own bag for candy. It was great! It wasn't until after we got home that I realized what had happened. I got to see fruit again. I got to see evidence in the lives of my children that what I am training them to do is working.

Without even knowing I was doing it, I gave them a test. I gave them a situation that required a number of things from all of them. They had to work together, work fast, cooperate, and take initiative, and the older ones had to look out for the younger ones. I offered them something they wanted (the parade) only if they made it possible for us to go. I had nothing to do with any of it. It was smooth and peaceful. It was good to see each of them put their best effort forward. It showed me what they are capable of doing, and it gave me some new ideas on how to motivate them.

Have you ever let your children do *all* of the preparations to go somewhere? It sure lets you know what they can do!

PRAYER

Lord, what a blessing it is to experience the joy that comes with observing children acting wisely. Help me to continue diligently training them to please You in their actions. They do learn. They are growing. Thank You that I have so much time to train them. ❧

FOOD FOR THOUGHT

1. Let your children do as much as possible as soon as possible. Good workers are developed early this way.
2. Praise your children when they act responsibly.
3. Rejoice in the fruit when it comes.

"WASTING TIME"

And Jesus answered and said unto her, Martha, Martha,
thou art careful and troubled about many things:
But one thing is needful: and Mary hath chosen that good part,
which shall not be taken away from her.

LUKE 10:41-42

This familiar passage of Scripture shows us that Jesus rebuked Martha for attending too much to the details and not spending more time listening to Jesus. I imagine that Martha's preoccupation with her work kept her from hearing the very truths from Jesus that could have helped her. Martha probably thought she was doing the right thing. After all, *somebody* had to take care of the preparations. She may not even have realized that she was out of balance until Jesus spoke to her about it.

How easy it is for us to fall into a similar trap. The laundry, the housecleaning, the food preparation and serving, and then homeschooling. The load we carry is staggering. Have you ever noticed that while the children are around you all day, you can reach evening without having had any meaningful dialogue with them? I can see that the details could swallow me every day and keep me from building relationships with my children that are important now.

Because I am task-oriented, I can become like Martha if I am not careful. I have learned to dialogue with my children while we work, and this helps some. But last Saturday I purposed to try something new. Even though I had planned to do many things, I set aside my "to do" list for the day. It was warm, and the children and I spent much time outdoors. In the afternoon I sat on a blanket with some of the children, and we just talked. Four-year-old Josiah spent some time with us after he fell off his bike and needed comforting. Little Julianne snuggled next to me for a while and then ran off to play. Jamie and I had some quality time to talk.

I thought about the day that evening as we were scurrying about cleaning up the house in time for unexpected guests who were coming with three hours' notice. I wondered if I would have been better off spending time during the day tidying the house. But the children and I were able to get the house in decent order in only an hour. Our time spent just being together in the afternoon in no way hampered me in the evening. We got done what mattered. It occurred to me that when I stop "doing" things and just start "being" Mom to my children, I am not wasting time. I am investing my time in building important relationships that need time. I can't just sandwich the children in between tasks. I felt good when I went to bed that night, knowing I had spent my time wisely.

Have you stopped and just played or talked to your children lately?

PRAYER

Father, thank You for showing me what matters. Help my schedule to reflect this understanding. ❧

FOOD FOR THOUGHT

1. Are you trapped by the thought that if you aren't doing something you are wasting time? Discard it now, and go play with your children.
2. Schedule in time in the day to "be" instead of "do."
3. Ask your children if they would like to spend more time talking and playing with you.

5 4

MEMORIZE IT

The law of his God is in his heart; none of his steps shall slide.

PSALM 37:31

❧

I am grateful that I have committed some Bible verses to memory. Saved in my late twenties, I did not have a childhood with memorizing Scripture as a part of my life. Consequently I have been learning as an adult. My Bible is highlighted and has many notes. Frequently Scripture is read, and I am familiar with it and can anticipate the next words as they are spoken. This, however, is not enough.

I can see the value in memorizing Bible verses. Psalm 46:10 ("Be still, and know that I am God") and Psalm 51:10 ("Create in me a clean heart, O God; and renew a right spirit within me") are two passages I pray often. I am comforted by them both. I can see the need to memorize more verses so they are in my heart and readily available to me at any time. If this is true for me, how much more important it is for my children to know verses that help them.

Psalm 37:4 ("Delight thyself also in the LORD; and he shall give thee the desires of thine heart") is an excellent verse for young people who are not dating. As they keep their hearts and bodies pure, waiting for God's best for them, they can be encouraged by this verse. It gives them specific direction about what to do. While waiting for a mate, they are to delight themselves in the Lord. Scripture is the true source of comfort, and we must help our children discover this source of blessing.

Just this morning at breakfast Jim shared Matthew 12:36-37 because many of us in the family have not been speaking to each other in a way that is honoring to God. Jesus said, "But I say unto you, That every idle word that men shall speak, they shall give account thereof in the day of judgment. For by thy words thou shalt be justified, and by thy words thou shalt be condemned." After talking about this verse together, our family communication improved. Scripture reminds us of the right ways to deal with people, circumstances, and life. It is our guide in times of trouble. Scripture is the source of direction for specific needs. Scripture is the answer to our questions.

Have you learned a new verse lately?

PRAYER

Dear Lord, help me to learn more Scripture. Show me how to make this a higher priority. Thank You for the comfort that the verses I know bring me daily. Show me how to teach my children the value of hiding Your Word in their hearts. Thank You for challenging me to do a better job. ✑

FOOD FOR THOUGHT

1. Make it a goal to learn a new Bible verse each month with your children.
2. Consider memorizing a larger portion of Scripture as a family. Consider the Gospel of John. Children who memorize something this demanding become adults who are confident they can do it.
3. Be creative with the younger ones. We used a deck of ABC Bible memory cards. We would put one card on top of the napkins at a time. A verse had to be recited before taking a napkin. The verses were simple, and we taught them out loud. Scripture memory became a natural part of our mealtime.

55

Words Matter

She openeth her mouth with wisdom; and in her tongue is the law of kindness.

PROVERBS 31:26

There are so many opportunities to speak unkindly in a homeschooling family, it scares me. I can never be too careful when it comes to the words I choose to speak to my husband and children. Often how we say something has more impact than the words themselves. We must mean what we say and say what we mean—all tempered by kindness.

One day I returned home late in the evening after taking a day for myself. While Jim ran the household, I ran some errands, did some shopping, and thoroughly enjoyed the refreshing quiet. By the end of the day I felt revived and renewed. I was ready to take on my responsibilities again.

Less than half an hour after entering the house, I found myself entangled with my daughter over some issue we had been working on for a long time. Having just finished a low-stress, peaceful day, I should have been able to handle the situation calmly and appropriately, but I did not. Instead I allowed myself to become annoyed at her behavior and let it escalate to the place where I said words that I regretted as soon as they left my mouth.

Before bed I apologized for my unkind words and asked forgiveness. My daughter was upset, and I felt like a failure—*again*. It is so easy to *react* to people and situations in your home when the right thing to do is to *respond*.

Let's face it—the behavior of children can rattle your nerves. It can push your buttons. It will try your patience. But who is the good example here? It ought to be you. I have noticed a tendency that I have to get caught up in the moment and forget about the big picture. Many, if not most, things looked at in terms of the big picture are not so distressing. I am committed to learning how to shut off my emotions that react and instead work out of my emotions that are calm and peaceful. Solutions rarely come from a frazzled mother anyway.

Did you react today or respond?

PRAYER

Lord, thank You for victory in this area today. Josiah wore a new shirt outside and rode his bike through mud puddles, splashing his back with mud. As I caught myself getting ready to react, I started to respond instead. I sent him upstairs to change and met him in his bedroom. I calmly explained that when he is wearing good clothes, he must change before playing outside. He smiled and sweetly said to me, "Mom, just remember that I won't be doing this again." I was completely unruffled. I put the shirt in the washer immediately, and the stains miraculously came out. Thank You for showing me how easy this can be with Your grace. ⇒

FOOD FOR THOUGHT

1. When there is a problem, do you react or think a minute and respond? If you react, what do you need to change right away? (Hint: Don't talk at all for at least five minutes after the incident.)
2. Would your children say that out of your mouth flows wisdom and kindness? What would your husband say?
3. Find someone to watch who is kind. Copy his or her style until kindness becomes a habit of your own.

5 6

WHO IS IN CONTROL?

And he commanded the multitude to sit down on the grass, and
took the five loaves, and the two fishes, and looking up to heaven,
he blessed, and brake, and gave the loaves to his disciples, and
the disciples gave them to the multitude. And they did all eat,
and were filled: and they took up of the fragments
that remained twelve baskets full.

MATTHEW 14:19-20

The end of our toothpaste tube is a mess. Toothpaste crusts over the end, and sometimes it is hard to even get the toothpaste out of the tube. I know, if we had the cap on, it wouldn't happen. Try to tell this to seven children. I used to, but I gave up.

Usually someone would leave the cap off anyway, and so I have accepted that at this stage of life our toothpaste is crusty. For some reason I have been able to use the toothpaste even though cleaning the end of the tube is gross. I just gave up on this one and moved on. It seems like such a little thing, but it is the small irritations of life that usually do the most damage.

Other sources of irritation are not so easily accepted. Toys left out seem to particularly irritate my husband. With seven children, I struggle with so many things getting broken. Other moms feel they can never get a grip on their laundry or food preparations that affect them daily. How much of this can we change? Certainly streamlining in all possible areas can help.

Realistically, we are best off to do all we can and then rest in knowing that some circumstances won't change in this season of life unless the Lord chooses to change them.

As the disciples saw the multitude of 5,000 needing to be fed, they went to Jesus wishing to send the people away to get their food. Jesus had other plans. Five loaves and two fishes fed them all, with some left over! The power Jesus has to change circumstances is available for you too. Homeschooling brings challenges that aren't always what you would choose to embrace. God knows. He is allowing these circumstances in your life for a reason. Let Him have His way in your circumstances, and you may see a miracle!

Is there something that needs to be done that seems too much for you? Ask Jesus.

PRAYER

Dear God, thank You for the powerful examples that You give us in your Gospels. The account in Matthew of the loaves and fishes shows me how finite my thinking is compared to Your power. Please work miracles in our family. Don't let us be limited by what my own eye can see. ❧

FOOD FOR THOUGHT

1. Are there things in your life that are overwhelming you? When you can see no possible way circumstances can work out favorably, remember the loaves and the fishes. The disciples never really knew how they ended up with enough food. They just did. Jesus can do the same for you. Just ask.
2. Are your children aware of the miracles that happen in the life of your family? Point out every one to them, no matter how small.
3. Pray for a childlike faith that believes God can do anything.

5 7

A COMPASSIONATE WIFE

Be ye therefore merciful, as your Father also is merciful.

LUKE 6:36

❧

Showing mercy to someone who disappoints us isn't always easy, but Jesus reminds us that we have been shown mercy already by the Father. Mercy is compassion for someone when they do something wrong. It is also the disposition to be merciful. As God is merciful to me, I am to be merciful to others. That's how it is supposed to work anyway. I have trouble with this when it is Jim who needs mercy.

Jim is highly distractible. He has been since I met him at age fifteen and likely will always have this quality. Often I have not had compassion for him in this area because I could not accept his distractibility. Since I am not distractible, I figured he should be able to "fix it." At least three of our children are distractible, and teaching them at home is showing me that it is difficult to "fix it." It may be that giving them tools to help them focus will improve their situation, but they may always fight some degree of distractibility. So what about a man in midlife who hasn't fully developed strategies to deal with his distractibility? He needs a merciful wife.

One of the ways this quality surfaces in Jim is the way he walks away without a word, and nobody knows where he is or whether he has any of the younger children with him. He will see something or remember something he has to do and just goes off and does it. Since his work schedule allows for him to be home during our school hours, this disruption is challenging. Sometimes twenty minutes will pass before I realize some of the children are missing. I have to find Jim, find the children, and then try to get everyone focused again.

This used to make me angry. I believed that he did not care how disruptive his behavior was to our school time. Only recently, after almost nineteen years of marriage, I learned that he doesn't even realize what he is doing. He gets distracted, focuses on the distraction, and forgets everything else. I now am learning to be merciful to him and to help him in this area. When I find him we smile because we both know it happened again. I am learning to have compassion for this weakness as God has compassion for my weak areas.

Is someone needing your compassion today?

PRAYER

Heavenly Father, I want to be merciful as You are merciful. I know I fall far short in this area. Help me to be compassionate when others struggle or have made a mistake. I am humbled as I think of my own weaknesses. I pray that my family would show me mercy as You have shown them mercy. ❧

FOOD FOR THOUGHT

1. Memorize Luke 6:36 as a family. Study the word *mercy* so that everyone understands what it means.
2. Are you recalling a time when you did not show mercy to someone? Make it right with him or her today.
3. Make a list of your weaknesses. As you look over it, let God soften you in the way you treat others. Let Him develop compassion and mercy in you. Know that this will bless others.

58

LEARNING THE LETTER SOUNDS

I press toward the mark for the prize of the high calling
of God in Christ Jesus.

PHILIPPIANS 3:14

*M*y sixth child, Josiah, is now learning to read. At four years old his eagerness continues to push me to teach him more. On his own he learned the alphabet, how to write all of the capital letters, and many of the letter sounds over a couple of months. Now he works with me in a first-grade phonics workbook. He surprises me as he understands more than I thought he would at this time. I anticipate that putting the sounds together and reading will come quickly for him. He started slowly, but soon his progress will be rapid.

How interesting the relationship is between learning to read and exercise—both physically and spiritually. For the first time ever, over the winter I was getting an hour of aerobic exercise (walking on a treadmill) four or five days per week. I felt great! At the beginning I found it taxing to walk for half an hour. Gradually I worked up to forty-five minutes and finally an hour. There have been many times in the past where I just gave up trying to exercise regularly. So I did not experience the benefits of regular exercise. My problem was stopping before mastering the basics of self-discipline. Imagine how difficult learning to read would be if we allowed our children to stop when it seemed too difficult or progress was too slow.

Spiritual exercise follows the same pattern. Establishing a daily routine (habit) for studying God's Word can be difficult and discouraging at the beginning. We may become frustrated and stop trying. The problem is that if you don't persevere through learning self-discipline, you won't achieve success.

I am still learning. It is summer now. I have fallen off of my exhilarating exercise program that I found easy to be faithful to in the winter. Our schedule is loosely structured this summer, and we are happy with more relaxed days. But my daily Bible time is not doing so well. With no regular place in our routine, it has become hit or miss. It would be easy to get discouraged since I had the self-discipline for both physical and spiritual exercise recently. Instead I am trying to walk thirty minutes per day three times a week on the treadmill during the summer. While this is a much reduced workout plan, it is still a goal. I am finishing a Bible study so I can do a new one with my older daughters this summer. We won't do it every day, but this also is a goal.

Are you frustrated with slow progress in your spiritual life? Press on!

PRAYER

Father, I appreciate the analogy between learning the letter sounds and reading and developing basic self-discipline for physical and spiritual exercise. Help me in the place where this analogy breaks down. When my children learn to read, they keep on reading. Please help me to keep the self-discipline of daily spiritual exercise once I have it. Don't let me lose this again. ❧

FOOD FOR THOUGHT

1. How is your self-discipline in daily Bible reading? Start small (five minutes per day), and establish a daily pattern.
2. Consider the benefits of filling yourself with God's Word daily. How can you homeschool without it?
3. Make time with God your spiritual priority for each day.

59

PERFECT PEACE

Thou wilt keep him in perfect peace, whose mind is stayed on thee:
because he trusteth in thee.

ISAIAH 26:3

❧

*I*t is common in our church to sing a few verses of Scripture before prayer
in the beginning moments of our Sunday morning service. Whenever we sing
these words from Isaiah I get uneasy. My mind wanders to the noise and distractions that are a part of each school day. When was the last time I had
perfect peace? Have I ever experienced this while juggling the needs of seven
children in our homeschool?

I am convicted that I have not. Why? The verse tells me. My mind must
be stayed on God *and* I must trust Him. Often I respond to the minute-to-
minute needs of finding lost pencils, teaching little ones to get along with each
other, and keeping everything going so we can be ready to eat on time. Oh
yes, I have to make provision (planning, buying food, cooking, serving, clear-
ing the table, washing dishes) for three meals a day too. So much to do, so
little time.

If I fail to keep my mind stayed on God, these many details will overwhelm me. My patience will be gone, and I will be unable to properly deal
with the spiritual and emotional needs of my family throughout the day.
Trusting in God keeps my mind focused on Him. It is God who sovereignly
orchestrates our school days. As we make schedules, keep calendars, and

organize our time, God knows what is in store for us each day. If we trust His plan, we have the grace to step back and deal with whatever comes our way each day.

"Perfect peace." What a role model I could be. If my children see this in me, my influence on them will be greater in all aspects of their lives. If I am frazzled and out of control, where will they learn to keep their mind on God amidst the daily difficulties they face in their own lives?

Are you a model of perfect peace to your family? I am not yet either.

PRAYER

Dear Jesus, this is very humbling for me to write. I can see that I have not applied this truth very well in my life. I can see how beneficial this would be, but applying this simple thought has been hard for me. Please help my mind to be stayed on You at all times. When I trust You and keep my mind stayed on You, You promise to keep me in perfect peace. Please help me to get this right. ❧

FOOD FOR THOUGHT

1. What takes away your peace each day? Focus your mind on God at these times and see what happens.
2. Consider the simplicity of this verse. It has the three following points: Keep your mind stayed on God because you trust Him, and He will keep you in perfect peace. If you do not have peace, determine if you really do trust God. If you don't trust Him, seek to understand why and deal with it.
3. Be encouraged that we can stay calm amidst the noise and distractions of our homeschool days. God has made provision for this if only we will follow His direction.

6 0

GOD IS THE POWER

That your faith should not stand in the wisdom of men,
but in the power of God.

1 CORINTHIANS 2:5

I was relieved when I heard the same doctor's name favorably mentioned twice in four days. Two months earlier I had suffered through my fifth miscarriage in eighteen months. I knew it was time for us "to do something" but had no clue regarding a specialist who could help me. Now I had made an appointment for Jim and me to speak to the specialist for one hour. Both of us were relieved because we felt this doctor could give us some answers.

The appointment was a month away, which gave me time to think. What would he find? What would he say? What if there was nothing conclusive? My flesh could dwell on these thoughts for days. Worry, fear, and a host of other emotions could easily consume me. Having miscarried so many times after having seven healthy children raised a lot of questions. Nobody had answers, and each time I became pregnant and miscarried, I had hormonal fluctuations that adversely affected daily life. Finally there was someone who understood what I was going through.

But I had to be careful to keep the role of the doctor in the proper perspective. Jim and I believe that God opens and closes the womb. Many verses have led us to believe this to be true. First Corinthians 2:5 is a verse I never before considered in relation to my womb. My faith is in "the power of God," not in "the wisdom of men." Doctors can guide us, but ultimately God performs the miracle of each new life He brings into the world. Whether or not the doctor can diagnose a problem with me or not does not affect God's power.

No matter what the outcome of the consultation with the doctor, God is the power. My faith is stretched as I am being forced by my circumstances to acknowledge who God is and to let Him have His way with me. Who other than a sovereign God would place me in a situation where His power can overrule earthly wisdom?

Is your faith being tested? Are you realizing that God is the power?

PRAYER

Dear Lord, I don't understand why I keep losing babies. As much as I would like a doctor to fix all of this, I know that it is You who has power over these circumstances. Help me to keep my focus on You and off the doctor. If I should miscarry again, help me to remember that You are the Sovereign One who allows such things to happen. I don't understand, but I trust You. I don't like this, but please help me to learn what I am supposed to through this trial. ঞ

FOOD FOR THOUGHT

1. Is there something in your life that is troubling you? Have you sought counsel from godly people? Balance good counsel with the understanding that it is the power of God that works the miracles. Allow troubling times to bring you closer to Jesus.
2. Put 1 Corinthians 2:5 on a 3 x 5 index card, and post it prominently in your home.
3. When trouble comes, is your first inclination to seek out someone to talk to about it? Try praying and seeking God's counsel first.

6 1

DRIP, DRIP, DRIP

A continual dropping in a very rainy day and
a contentious woman are alike.

PROVERBS 27:15

❧

I don't care much for this verse. It reminds me too much of myself. A cursory reading doesn't give you the full ramifications of the verse. But read this on a rainy spring day when the rain comes down all day long. Listen to the raindrops. It can get on your nerves. It doesn't take long before you want to get away from the rain.

A "contentious woman" is the same. People want to get away from her. The word *contentious* sounds bad. We don't want to be like that! But what does it mean? A contentious woman is one with a wearisome tendency to engage in quarrels. She is apt to arouse conflict because she has a marked difference of opinion—and she lets you know it.

There is such a fine line that we walk as mothers directing our children in our homes and as wives allowing our husbands to give direction. When Jim comes home from work, I let him take over again as the leader in our home. He delegates the job to me while he is at work, but it is his when he returns home. We need to have a blending time when I fill him in on children and situations. After he has been briefed, he is more effective with the family. If he takes over without the blending time, the results are interesting. The children may balk at his direction and look to me for help since "Dad doesn't understand."

I don't like to be caught in this position. Blending time is critical; if it is missed, I can be on the verge of becoming a contentious woman. If I choose at that time to point out how things should be handled differently, I am expressing a marked difference of opinion with my husband in front of my children. It is easy for them to take sides, and you don't ever want this to happen. The best remedy I have found is to be quiet and to allow my husband to approach me later. The more I practice this, the more Jim is drawn to talk to me about this transition time when he comes home from work.

Do you give your husband back his rightful leadership in the home when he returns from work?

PRAYER

Father, I don't want to be "a contentious woman." Help me to wait for Jim to ask for my opinion instead of voicing it so freely. Help us with our blending time when he comes home from work, so this transition will be smoother. When it does not go so well, help me to be meek and humble instead of offering instruction on how to do it better. Show me the best way to be a help to my husband. ❧

FOOD FOR THOUGHT

1. Is your husband the leader in your home? Do you need to step back and allow him to fill his God-given role?
2. Consider keeping your opinions to yourself until your husband asks you to share them. It may take time before he asks, but eventually he will want to know why you are so quiet.
3. Which is more important—that your opinions are heard and considered or that your children have a model of a sweet-spirited wife and mother?

6 2

LET'S GET ORGANIZED

Let all things be done decently and in order.

1 CORINTHIANS 14:40

*H*omeschooling is easier if you are organized. I am grateful that I naturally tend toward being organized. When disorder creeps in, I can handle it
up to a point, but then I need to stop and put things back together. This is
necessary and good, but this is not enough. If my organizational skills were
the only ones that mattered in our home, things would be pretty smooth.
But a husband and many children affect the organization in our home.

Keeping myself organized is pretty easy for me. But my job includes
making sure that my children are orderly. They need to know how to get
themselves organized and then stay organized. They need tools such as a
daily planner and accountability that asks them if they used their planner.
They need alarm clocks that they set to wake up on time. They need deadlines and need to follow through to be sure they meet their deadlines. They
need to learn to set goals and then make plans to reach them. Sounds easy,
doesn't it? Well . . .

Not all of my children think this organizing business is much fun. Each
child has a plastic crate to keep his or her books and supplies in, but a
couple of them can't seem to keep the books inside the crate. They waste
time looking for lost books. Some of my children can't wait until they are
old enough to have a planner. Others don't know where they set it down

last. Alarm clocks work well, but only for the children who set them. The naturally organized are frustrated by the disorderly. This surely is a good training opportunity.

Good organizing skills are beneficial for a lifetime. Orderliness is a good testimony. God desires for us to be organized. For some it will be easier than for others. Either way, it is up to us to make sure our children receive training in this vital area. They need to learn to coexist with people who are more or less organized than they are. The less organized need to see how their disorganization negatively impacts those around them. The very organized need to see that some people can't maintain their high organizational standards without being stressed. It is a question of balance in the area of organization. What a blessing that our home environment with children with different organizing styles gives us a natural opportunity for training.

Are your children learning to be orderly?

PRAYER

Heavenly Father, thank You for gifting me with organization. You have allowed me to teach my own children how to be orderly, and there is fruit. Thank You that You have shown me how important this life skill is to the future success of each one of my children. Help me to be sensitive to the unique needs of each child in this area. ❧

FOOD FOR THOUGHT

1. Are you organizationally challenged? Pick up a copy of *The Busy Mom's Guide to Simple Living* by Jackie Wellwood (Crossway Books, 1997).
2. As you train for organization, praise good attitudes and efforts more than perfect task completion. Starting children young will instill right attitudes even when their performance is still limited.
3. Is there some aspect of your home (in addition to their bedrooms) that you could assign to each child that he or she could be completely responsible to keep organized?

6 3

LESSON PLANS

Thou wilt show me the path of life: in thy presence is fulness of joy;
at thy right hand there are pleasures for evermore.

PSALM 16:11

❧

The term *lesson plans* is a carryover from school days when we were children. Teachers had lesson plans so they knew what to do each day and also so a substitute teacher could come in and take over without much disruption. I also make a type of lesson plan that outlines what books each child will cover and how many pages should be covered each week, so we will all be finished at the same time. The funny thing is that this has never happened as planned. There have not been any substitute teachers knocking at my door either.

So why plan anyway? So many things come up to alter my plans that some school years barely resemble my initial vision for that year. It's not really the lesson plans that are a problem. Who makes the plans is the key. My understanding of the needs of my children is limited without God. While I know what I believe I should cover each year, God knows what He wants me to cover and when. Only by prayerful consultation with the Sovereign One will my lesson plans be approved.

Interruptions to the schedule are often divine appointments. We have flexibility as homeschoolers to help the needy on weekdays along with our children. We can open our homes to others as a family. If we cling too tightly to our own lesson plans, we will miss out on the divine opportunities God provides us. Many of us still remember the tedious six-hour days sitting behind a desk bored to tears. When we are having fun in our homeschooling, it can almost seem like we are playing hooky. When we break from our plans to help someone, it may seem like we are taking off from school. On the contrary, that is school. Allowing our children to learn to serve others is part of the curriculum.

When we are in God's will, the verse promises "joy" and "pleasures." Homeschooling can be hard, but it is not hopeless. When God directs and we follow, in His "presence" we find "fullness of joy" and "pleasures for evermore."

Who is directing your homeschool?

PRAYER

Dear God, thank You for being the source of all things. I don't have to rely on myself to figure out the plans for the school year. Show me what You would desire for each of our children. Guide me as I select books and work up a plan for the year. Help me to see Your divine "interruptions," so that I may rejoice in them. Don't let me miss the joy and pleasure that are part of homeschooling. ❧

FOOD FOR THOUGHT

1. If you don't make any specific plans for your school year, consider doing so now. Without plans, it is difficult to know how much time you need and how much time you can use to take on new projects.
2. What do you consider as you make plans for the school year? Is service either in the church or in the community a part of your plan?
3. Do you schedule your year leaving some "free" time in case God has other plans during the year? How flexible are you to make changes as opportunities come up?

6 4

WHAT ARE YOU THINKING ABOUT?

Finally, brethren, whatever things are true, whatever things are honest,
whatever things are just, whatever things are pure,
whatever things are lovely, whatever things are of good report;
if there be any virtue, and if there be any praise,
think on these things.

PHILIPPIANS 4 : 8

Jim has a way of communicating with me that makes me crazy. I'm serious. He will say something in a way that communicates something completely different from what he means. Usually this turns out sounding negative. I interpret it as mean. I have tried to overlook this, but sometimes it completely wears me down.

The last couple of years have been difficult for us. It was during this time that I developed the thought, *He is mean.* Every time we don't communicate well and what he says is even slightly negative, I remind myself, *He is mean.* I get upset much more easily because of this thought pattern. Many times the best response from me would have been to overlook the words that he was saying without taking them personally. I have noticed that negative words launched at me are often an attempt to cover up something he said or did. It wasn't really about me at all.

We must program our minds to think right thoughts. Making a habit of remembering the good in a person helps us during the times when communication isn't so good. It helps us to respond properly rather than reacting. Reminding ourselves of praiseworthy behavior in the past helps us to cope with present behavior that is troubling.

As wives and mothers we cannot afford to develop negative attitudes toward our husbands or our children. Daily disappointments can be worked through by a sweet and gentle wife and mother. It will be much more difficult if we allow the negative to dominate our minds with a "one strike against them" mentality. It takes conscious effort and continuing work to cultivate positive thoughts. But what we put into our minds directly affects the health of our soul. And a healthy soul in a homeschooling wife and mother is certain to be pleasing to God.

What are you thinking about?

PRAYER

Lord, I appreciate the understanding You have given me regarding how my thoughts affect my actions. Help me to think positively of my husband, so that when what he says isn't exactly what he means, I won't be offended by it. Help me to always give the benefit of the doubt when Jim says things that seem mean to me. The health of my soul doesn't depend upon what people say to me, but how I respond to their words. Let me be gracious in my responses, made possible by a heart filled with things that are true, honest, just, pure, lovely, of good report, virtuous, and praiseworthy. ❧

FOOD FOR THOUGHT

1. When your husband says things that rub you the wrong way, how do you respond? Is your first thought that he meant it that way or that maybe he just did not communicate well?
2. What thoughts fill your mind? Do you choose to think of good or bad?
3. Thinking good thoughts can help you weather the storms that sometimes come in relationships. Even if the other person was being mean, your soul fares better when you think the best of him or her.

6 5

WHAT DID YOU SAY?

Death and life are in the power of the tongue: and they that love it
shall eat the fruit thereof.

PROVERBS 18:21

❧

One morning I was helping four-year-old Josiah with his breakfast. He wanted some cereal from an unopened box, and I could see that he was having some trouble. "Can I open up the cereal for you, big guy?" I asked. "Yes, you can, big Mama," he replied. Josiah didn't think twice about what he said since it sounded so similar to what I had just said to him.

Our sons and daughters are modeling us all of the time. What we do, how we act, and particularly what we say gives them an example. Young children take words literally and have trouble understanding the subtle differences in communication. Even if what we say isn't what we really mean, it is what they model. If we have a critical spirit toward others in our church, it will be reflected in the way our children relate to people at church. They watch us and pick up what we teach them by our example. If we mutter under our breath when things don't suit us, we teach them to be disrespectful.

Our tone of voice means perhaps even more to our children than our words. When they are disobedient, do we talk harshly to them, or is the law of kindness on our lips? How do we speak to our husband? How do we answer the telemarketer who calls during dinner? Our lives are open books to our children, who know us better than we might like them to. They can hear one sentence spoken with the wrong tone of voice and know if we are upset, tired, or angry. Knowing we are under the magnifying glass should motivate us to be more careful about what we say and how we say it.

Our tongues are part of our curriculum. There is no charge and no storage. It is always there and never gets used up. Those are pretty good criteria for curriculum. Powerful beyond our comprehension, our tongue should be life to our children. Our words and tone of voice should be an encouragement to them. Our tongues can communicate truth, direction, love, and more. They also can be destructive. Let it be the power of life that is on the tongue of the homeschool mother.

How is your tongue doing today?

PRAYER

Dear Lord, prompt me when my tongue is not pleasing to You. It is so easy to say the wrong things in the wrong tone of voice when I am talking with children for thirteen- to fourteen-hour stretches each day. Help me to see my bad attitude before it goes too far. Let me be a good example with my tongue. Help me to practice what I tell the children: "If you don't have anything good to say, don't say anything." Thank You for continuing to refine my character. ❦

FOOD FOR THOUGHT

1. Do you see yourself in your children? Do you like what you see? Could you make changes in what you model before them that would improve the situation?
2. Pay attention to your tone of voice. Our children can learn to talk exactly like we do. Let it be a proper tone of voice they learn from us.
3. Ask your children to forgive you when you are a poor example in this area.

PASS THE TEST

Beloved, think it not strange concerning the fiery trial which is to try you, as though some strange thing happened unto you.

1 PETER 4:12

❧

The words *meek* and *quiet* have been stumbling blocks for me for years. Although I very much desire these qualities in my life, I find that proud and loud come easier to me. One day I set out to fix this once and for all. I worked on a Bible study for one month to see what I could learn. *Putting on a Gentle and Quiet Spirit* by Elizabeth George was filled with practical ways for me to both understand and apply the character qualities of meekness and quietness in my life. I felt pretty good about what I was learning (that sounds proud, doesn't it?).

I filled in the answers in the book just fine. But I wasn't ready for the tests. You see, the Bible study did not contain any tests. Situations kept coming up where people were rubbing me the wrong way. A couple of individuals were nasty to me. I found myself with a daily supply of circumstances where the right response was meekness and quietness. By the last week of the study I determined to hurry up and finish so the tests would stop. At least I thought they would.

The day after my last lesson was truly a final exam. In four hours I had four opportunities. The first one was responding meekly and quietly to my husband whose words over the telephone were provoking me. I got this one wrong. Next, I was entering a situation where I had every reason to believe I would be chastised for something beyond my control. Praying for God's grace to keep me calm and quiet, I entered the situation and nothing happened. This one was easy.

The next two were unexpected and observed by my two oldest daughters. I was sharing a problem with someone who just laughed at me. I walked away without a word! Score! Lastly, I had some difficulty checking into a hotel and finally decided I would go to another one. Before I could ask how I had handled the conflict, my oldest, Jamie, told me I had been meek. Praise God for even just a little progress!

Are you known for your meek and quiet spirit?

PRAYER

Dear Lord, the training ground of life that develops a meek and quiet spirit is difficult. Thank You that I have had some success, even though I still fall short of what You desire for me. Thank You for granting me understanding, and now I pray for help in the application of what I have learned. I desire for my daughters to learn how to respond correctly from their mother. Please help me soon so I don't keep getting this wrong! ❧

FOOD FOR THOUGHT

1. Have you ever thought that when we are trying to learn something new in the Christian life, we can expect God to test us to see if we are getting the material?
2. How do you respond to failed tests? Go on and try again. In some areas it may take many tests before we pass. Perseverance produces results. Quitting is guaranteed failure.
3. Ask your husband periodically if you are meek and quiet. If he never says "Yes," work on it more. If he says "Sometimes," be encouraged by your progress.

67

BAN SATAN FROM SCHOOL

*Be sober, be vigilant; because your adversary the devil,
as a roaring lion walketh about, seeking whom he may devour.*

1 PETER 5:8

We believe in sheltering our children. We don't need to teach them about the evils of this world along with phonics and math. They will taste the "real world" soon enough, as they mature into young adults. Armed with a solid faith and an answer for what they believe, they will be ready to face the world at that time. We don't completely *isolate* our children, but we *insulate* them from what is not good for them.

Satan is having a field day with today's young people. Secular humanism has paved the way for explicit teaching on drugs, immorality, alternative lifestyles, and more as common fare in our public schools. Teach children how to indulge in sin, and Satan doesn't have to do much to see that those kids are lost.

But what about *our* children? If we are shielding them from the filth of this world, how will Satan get our children? If he can't destroy them from without (exposure to worldly evils), he will seek to devour them from within (the family). As we spend our days together as families educating at home, we can get on each other's nerves. Minor irritations turn into major blowouts, and we no longer have unity in our family. Satan is at work here, just as he is outside the home. The difference is in how we fight Satan inside and out.

We insulate from outside influences that are bad by not allowing them into our home. We insulate from the inside with prayer.

No amount of prayer would be too much for a homeschool. We must be vigilant daily to watch for any areas in our family life where we are letting Satan gain a foothold within our home. Disobedience and bad attitudes should be dealt with quickly. Disrespect must be addressed immediately. Use your imagination, and see how many things that go on in your home could be an opening for Satan to dismantle your family. Strong homeschooling families that are built upon the Word of God are a threat to the secular humanism that drives our country. If we are successful, God will get the glory. Certainly Satan will try anything to prevent us from reaching our goals. Be sure to banish Satan from your school daily.

Does Satan have any ground in your family?

PRAYER

Father, help me to stay near to You. It is so easy to miss things that give Satan a door into my home. I don't want there to be any doors, windows, or even cracks in my house that let Satan in to harm our family. God, help me to see and understand the dangers that lurk within our home. Please show me how to work through problems as they arise so that we may be a united family. ❧

FOOD FOR THOUGHT

1. Pick up a copy of Jim Logan's *Reclaiming Surrendered Ground: Protecting Your Family from Spiritual Attacks* (Moody Press, 1995).
2. Use your freedom to pray in your school often.
3. Resist the devil, and he will flee from you. Don't forget that he is there and is walking around trying to find a way into your family. Don't give him one.

6 8

$mε$, $HOMεSCHOOL$?

Commit thy works unto the LORD, and
thy thoughts shall be established.

PROVERBS 16:3

◦⁂

*I*t is not every woman who sets out to homeschool with joy in her heart and a song on her lips. For many, fear and trembling better describes how she feels. That was me. It wasn't my idea to homeschool. It was my husband's. When my older girls were three and one year old, Jim announced that we should homeschool. It sounded like it was already decided, and I didn't know what to think. I wasn't sure I wanted to even try it.

I had more questions than answers and only knew of one family that homeschooled. I called them, and then I read a book at their recommendation. *A Survivor's Guide to Home Schooling* by Luanne Shackelford and Susan White gave me a vision. I sensed that I could probably do it. I still wasn't too excited though. It seemed like a lot of work (it is), and I had much to learn. But Jim wanted me to do it, and I was becoming convinced that homeschooling was the best choice for our family. Many questions remained, but they were not to be answered before we started homeschooling.

Without the Lord, I don't know how I could have homeschooled. Much prayer has sustained me through twelve years of this challenging lifestyle. If I had waited for a peaceful tranquillity to fill my soul before I started, I probably would never have started at all. The decision was made to homeschool, and then we got started. As we committed this endeavor to the Lord, our thoughts did become established. We attended many conferences and workshops that taught us and encouraged us in our homeschooling. God continues to provide what we need to keep going.

Each year I face new challenges. With seven children ranging from preschool to high school, I feel stretched. But this work (homeschooling) has been committed to the Lord. On days when I'm not sure I can do this, He is there establishing my thoughts and enabling me to continue. The work is hard, and the rewards are great. God is faithful; so even if you start out not wanting to homeschool, it can all work out.

Are you excited about homeschooling or scared? Give your fears to God.

PRAYER

Father, some days I still don't feel like homeschooling. I know it is the right choice, but it demands so much of me. Establish my thoughts daily. Help me to be focused on what is important and to let the rest go. I can't do this without You. I want to enjoy homeschooling. Help me to have the balance in my life to juggle so many things. Keep me in the paths of Your choosing, and bring me back when I stray. ❧

FOOD FOR THOUGHT

1. What is your attitude toward homeschooling? Are you reluctant? Burned out? Apprehensive? Ready to quit? Give God a chance to establish your thoughts, and then see how you feel.
2. If you are a new homeschooler, find a veteran who can be a mentor to you. If you are a veteran, make time to encourage new homeschoolers. Remember how it felt when you were getting started.
3. Memorize Proverbs 16:3. Bring this to mind each time you get frustrated.

WAIT FOR THE FRUIT

Be patient therefore, brethren, unto the coming of the Lord.
Behold, the husbandman waiteth for the precious fruit of the earth,
and hath long patience for it, until he receive
the early and latter rain.

JAMES 5:7

❧

I wonder how many years it takes to successfully train young boys to put dirty clothes in the hamper instead of on the floor. My oldest son is ten, and we are still in training. I have tried many methods to help my three boys thrive, yet dirty clothes are still on the floor. One method I have not considered is time. I don't mean more time to pick up clothes. I mean time for the training to sink in and produce fruit.

We planted an orchard three years ago, and the trees are all healthy, but few are producing fruit yet. They are pruned each year, watered when needed, and staked so the wind does not hurt the young trees. When they are mature enough, they will bear fruit. The care we are giving the trees now will make a difference in how well the trees produce later.

This is true for my sons too. While I wonder sometimes if they are understanding what I am teaching about picking up dirty clothes, I can see that other things I have taught them they do understand. I can see the fruit. Just the other day all three of my boys demonstrated the character quality of initiative in the same day. Jimmy (age ten) decided on his own to carry his sisters' laundry baskets down two flights of stairs to the laundry area. Jonathan (age eight) began cleaning up toys in the living room without being asked. Josiah (age four) saw that we were one bowl short at the lunch table and went and got another one from the kitchen just as I was noticing the problem.

We have been teaching about taking initiative with a good attitude for years. I have wondered why the children seemed to need prompting so much of the time to do what needs to be done. But then here was a day where the fruit of this teaching came forth. I just had to wait. I had to be patient. Just as caring for our young orchard will yield fruit in the future, so will character training yield fruit in our children—in time.

Have you been waiting a long time for fruit? Keep your eyes open—you may see it anytime.

PRAYER

Dear Jesus, thank You for opening my eyes to the character displayed by my boys. I do so much correcting of them that I could miss the fruit if I am not careful. Help me to look past the areas where they are slow to learn, like dirty clothes on the floor. Let me be a mother who continually praises the fruit in her children. Thank You for teaching me to wait. ❧

FOOD FOR THOUGHT

1. List the areas in which your children do not seem to be learning. Then list areas where you have observed fruit. Be encouraged by the fruit you have seen. Keep training diligently, and watch as items on the first list get transferred to the second list.
2. Determine what matters most, and focus your training there. Be prepared to wait for results.
3. How long has God been waiting for your fruit? Don't be so hard on your children.

70

A BAD DAY

*Go from the presence of a foolish man, when thou perceivest not
in him the lips of knowledge.*

PROVERBS 14:7

❧

Who hasn't had a bad day? I have. So has my husband. He doesn't seem
like the man I married on such days. In fact, if he had been having very
many bad days when I met him, I might not have married him. Why not?
Because he is a completely different man on those days.

After nineteen years of marriage I am realizing that I really married two
men—Jim and the other guy, also named Jim, who sees things differently
when he has a bad day. Some days Jim is sleep-deprived from his firefight-
ing job and has a headache. If I am not aware of this, I try to communicate
with him just like I always do, but with the most interesting results. He may
lash out at me or blame me for something that is not my fault. I have been
reduced to tears on more than one occasion.

As a wife, I need to discern what kind of day my husband is having.
Certain topics should be held for a different day. On his bad days, I must build
him up and save "business" for another time. The less I require of him on
his bad days, the better it is for both of us. Much can be accomplished in a
little time on a good day. I have found that on a bad day, nothing I want to
address will be handled well anyway.

Children have bad days too. It might be that requiring less of them on a bad day would be profitable. Confronting them about problems with school-work, character, or work in the home on a bad day probably won't yield the results you are looking for. It could be that our sensitivity to our children on their bad days will encourage them even more than we know. Take their negative words and actions lightly on bad days. Encourage them, and then confront these words and actions in a positive way on their next good day.

Is anyone having a bad day at your house?

PRAYER

Father, thank You for giving me the wisdom to back off from my husband and children when they are having a bad day. Please help me do a better job of applying this wisdom. I pray that You would make my family sensitive to me when I have bad days. We can be such an encouragement to one another when we understand these needs. Let our home be a haven of rest where all of us are happy to be when we are having a bad day. ❧

FOOD FOR THOUGHT

1. Where can Mom go when she has a bad day? Make arrangements to get away for a day when you need it. A break is all we need to revive us much of the time.
2. When the whole family seems to be having a bad day, check the schedule. Does the family need a break? Spontaneously take a day trip to a museum or a zoo.
3. Be sensitive to each family member's day. Decide wisely which topics to discuss and which to deal with later. Save yourself a lot of relational headaches.

7 1

An Older Woman

*The aged women likewise, that they be in behavior as becometh
holiness, not false accusers, not given to much wine,
teachers of good things; that they may teach the young women
to be sober, to love their husbands, to love their children,
to be discreet, chaste, keepers at home, good, obedient to their
own husbands, that the word of God be not blasphemed.*

TITUS 2:3-5

It is good to have an older, godly woman who teaches you about God's desires
for your life. It helps to have an example of holiness to observe as you learn
which behaviors please God. I am encouraged when I am around older
women who are still excited about their children. Older women have a perspective on life that I don't have yet. How important it is to receive godly
instruction through the wisdom of an older woman.

A number of older women have helped me in different ways. One is a
friend of mine who lives in another state. She has written a book for women
on marriage, and when we converse on the phone, she always encourages
me with her wisdom coupled with a sensitive understanding of how I feel.
Another older woman, also out of state, is the mother of six children who
has a ministry of singing the praises of motherhood. A true cheerleader for
mothers, she has blessed me through her writing as well as through a retreat
that I attended. And an older woman in our church continues to be a source

of encouragement to me when I need help. Always available, she calmly helps me focus on what is most important—namely, how God sees a circumstance. Her ability to give me perspective during trials is unsurpassed.

Another older woman who has blessed me with her wisdom is my mother-in-law. One time while feeling intensely frustrated, I decided to call her for advice. This may sound scary to you, but if you have never done it, do it at least once—you may be pleasantly surprised. I figured that a mother would know her son well enough to be a help. She did not defend Jim but rather helped me to look for an underlying problem that was perpetuating our difficulties. I began to see things in a new light that clarified the underlying problem.

I praise God for my mother-in-law's sensitivity to me. In a calm, unruffled manner she let me talk through what I was feeling. She gently reminded me of the love my husband has for me. She encouraged me as she prayed that God would show me some answers. And He did in a matter of a few days. She blessed me by taking time to talk to me right when I needed it, to point me in the right direction even though she was in the midst of physical pain that was wearing her down. She was a good example to me.

Do you realize that you are the older woman in the life of your daughters?

PRAYER

Dear Jesus, thank You for Your provision of older, godly women to provide us with much needed examples. ❧

FOOD FOR THOUGHT

1. Seek out godly older women to mentor you.
2. Be teachable.
3. Thank God for the special way that women understand each other and can help each other to live holy lives.

72

A Sense of Humor

A time to weep, and a time to laugh; a time to mourn,
and a time to dance.

ECCLESIASTES 3:4

❧

*B*edtime is often an opportunity for parents to see creativity emerge in their children as they try new ways to stall the process. Brushing teeth, needing another drink, and using the bathroom are all ways that my younger children have stretched the bedtime routine. Since Jim works overnight at the fire station, on his workdays I am responsible to oversee this bedtime routine myself.

Some days I am so tired by the evening that I don't have much left to offer my children at bedtime. My tolerance for stalling techniques is low. Such was the case after passing the boys' room and finding four-year-old Josiah out of bed. "What are you doing?" I asked him. "I'm putting on my dress," he replied matter-of-factly. I just started laughing. Then he began to laugh too. What he meant was that he was getting dressed in his pajamas.

He saw his mistake and thought it was funny. What a powerful lesson my little guy taught me in the twilight of the day when I could easily have missed it. Laugh! When you make a mistake, laugh. Mistakes are made all of the time as we train our children in our homes. Taking our mistakes too seriously makes us feel like failures. We may set unrealistic performance standards for ourselves and then be convinced we aren't good enough when we don't measure up to the unattainable.

When nothing gets crossed off the "to do" list, laugh. When you only finish half the math book this year, laugh. When you pass by the wall with crayon marks on it, laugh. When you eat cereal for dinner because you didn't plan for dinner, laugh. Laugh at your shortcomings, oversights, and omissions. As you learn to laugh at yourself, you will find it easier to laugh at the problems created by others instead of becoming irritated.

How often do your children see you laughing?

PRAYER

Heavenly Father, I know that I take life too seriously. My six-year-old Joanna takes hardly anything seriously, and I notice that she is constantly smiling. What does she know that I don't? Help me to balance my focused, task-oriented seriousness with a more lighthearted approach to life. When the inevitable comes each day, let my first reaction to calamity be laughter. I sense that I would be more effective in dealing with daily issues if I would just laugh more. Please bring someone into my life who does this well. She would be a good influence on me. ❧

FOOD FOR THOUGHT

1. What type of personality do you have? The serious ones (melancholy) need to work at lightening up. The fun-loving ones (sanguine) might need to get a little more serious.
2. Learn about the personalities of your children. Read *Personality Plus for Parents—Understanding What Makes Your Child Tick* by Florence Littauer (Revell, 2000).
3. Enjoy stronger relationships as you learn how personality influences how you relate to each of your children and how they relate to you. Identify who needs to cultivate a sense of humor, and work on it. It will change the tone in your home.

73

What's on the Calendar?

Better is an handful with quietness, then both the hands full with travail and vexation of spirit.

ECCLESIASTES 4:6

I am amazed at how busy I am as a homeschool mom. Although I have much flexibility with my schedule, I must guard the calendar. Engaging in too many activities brings unwanted stress and pressure into our home. Even on the days when we never leave the farm, too many expectations for the day can cause problems for us.

We often think that getting a lot done is a sign of productivity. It can be. But not if there is tension and strife involved to get it all done. I regularly over-commit myself to work in my home. Yes, it needs to be done, but some of it should be left undone if the atmosphere in our home is tense. On some days necessity will dictate that much work be done. On other days there should be a balance of some time where getting things done is not the focus.

Sitting around and talking to your children is very productive. It is so enjoyable that it seems like you aren't accomplishing anything. But you are—possibly the very best thing you can do. Other tasks may go unfinished, but I would rather be surrounded by peaceful children whose mother spent time with them than get much accomplished with unruly children because Mom was too task-oriented.

As I write, it is summer. I like to get "caught up" during the summer. I like to work on projects that get neglected during the school year. Not this summer though. Finishing this book is the main task focus I have until the end of July. Throughout the finishing of the book I am spending time each day just being with my children. We are going to parks, going out for lunch, and planning other just-for-fun activities. We are bonding nicely. We aren't trying to reach productivity goals each day. We are getting to know each other better. We work hard during most of the year. We need some time to just enjoy each other this summer.

Balance is hard to achieve on a daily basis, but there is a way we can tell how we are doing. Is there a "quietness" about your home, or are you suffering from "vexation of spirit"? I don't know of many homeschoolers who do too little. Most of us do too much. Ease up a little, and enjoy your children. You won't regret it.

So what are you going to do for fun today?

PRAYER

Dear Lord, I want my children to remember me as being a "fun" mom. I can easily become absorbed by the work around me and forget to have fun. Help me to be balanced in my work and in my play. I don't want to raise children who become workaholics, but adults who understand balance and have it in their lives. Help us to learn balance together since what they learn in our home is what they will likely do in their own homes. ❧

FOOD FOR THOUGHT

1. Have you considered that your children will not naturally know how to balance work and play? Teach them to work hard but to allow some free time after the work is finished to just have fun.
2. Are you feeling stressed? Do you have any free time?
3. Be spontaneous. Play for a whole day!

7 4

WHAT DOES RESPECT LOOK LIKE?

Nevertheless let every one of you in particular so love his wife even as himself; and the wife see that she reverence her husband.

EPHESIANS 5:33

❧

Why, in the final analysis, do I bring on my own troubles? The Bible gives clear directions to me as a wife regarding my behavior and my attitudes toward my husband. I have studied these. I have taught them. I have purposed to apply them daily in my own life. They just haven't become a habit yet. I particularly struggle with reverencing my husband.

Reverence means respect. Humility, loyalty, and praise communicate this to my husband. As I show Jim respect, I am teaching my children how to do the same. A bad attitude or a complaining spirit brings a different result. It teaches my children to show their father disrespect. One day I was trying to help my oldest daughter with some difficulties she was having with her dad. I decided to give her some suggestions.

I told her that she needed to reverence her dad. She appropriately told me that I needed to do that too. Ouch, that hurt! But she was right. I had been a poor role model for her, and the results were disappointing. I humbled myself before her and asked forgiveness for my failure in this area. I told her that I wanted her to hold me accountable to reverence Jim. This is humbling, and I wouldn't have chosen this, but it is time to repair the wrong teaching I have given her by my example. As she learns to tactfully do this for me, she will be learning how to show respect for me too.

I really did not care to be so vulnerable with my daughter, but this very opportunity helped me to see some important work that I needed to do. No matter what is happening, God requires me to reverence my husband. I also humbled myself before my husband and confessed my lack of respect for him. He told me that if I get this right, the rest will fall in line. I believe him. Now I just need to have patience with the process.

Are your children learning respect from you?

PRAYER

Father, I need Your help. I have head knowledge but struggle to apply it properly in daily life. I haven't seen many women reverencing their husbands, and I honestly don't know what it looks like. Please show me how to show respect no matter what my husband says or does. Help me to ignore the many bad examples I see of women criticizing, belittling, and making fun of their husbands. I don't want to be like them or be influenced by them. Our generation needs to set a new standard, a godly standard, in reverencing our husbands. We need Your help desperately. ❧

FOOD FOR THOUGHT

1. Look up the word *reverence* in the dictionary. List behaviors and attitudes you have that are not showing reverence to your husband. Deal with these quickly since you know your children are watching you.
2. What is God's role in helping you show reverence to your husband? Ask Him for more grace.
3. Study the character quality of respect as a family. All family members need to show respect to each other. Make this a priority since this is the foundation required to learn other character qualities.

SHE REMEMBERED ME

*Pleasant words are as a honeycomb, sweet to the soul,
and health to the bones.*

PROVERBS 16:24

❧

I had to pick up some promotional pictures at a portrait studio and took the opportunity to take twelve-year-old Jenny along so she could have her portrait done. She had the same photographer that did my pictures. Upon seeing the two of us together, the photographer recalled the time over one year ago that our entire family had come into the studio. Amazed that she would remember perfect strangers after photographing hundreds of people, I was shocked by what she said next.

As I stood there and listened, she related to Jenny how I told the children to make silly faces after our "package" pictures were finished. I didn't want the extra shots to be good because they were more expensive. How did she remember I said that? She said it was no big deal because people say that type of thing all the time. No matter, I was still thinking about the impression my words left on a perfect stranger.

How much do my words really matter? They matter more than I can comprehend. This incident made me think that even when I am saying something negative, I need to use the most pleasant and positive words I can find. If people hear me and remember me in terms of the words I have spoken, then my image can be enhanced or destroyed by those words. Imagine how powerful this thought is as it relates to our children.

As we train our children in our homes, we have ample opportunity to leave a lasting impression. If we are bossy in the way we direct our children, it is unlikely that we will have a sweet effect on them. When troubles arise, as they will, we must choose "pleasant words" to redirect our children to the correct path. We must choose to model respect by the words we choose. At the portrait studio I showed no respect for the way they set up their packages. While getting a good discount on a package, part of the program is to have them take additional pictures that they hope you will want to buy too. That is the way they do it, and I should have just let it go. By my comments I was teaching my children to be disrespectful. This year when we had our family pictures taken, they were the best ever. I never said a word.

What impression are your words leaving?

PRAYER

Dear Jesus, the power of my words scares me. I am appalled that a stranger remembered what I said for over a year when I thought nothing of my words. Please help me to be more careful and to think before I speak. Remind me of the power of every word spoken. Teach me how to address unpleasant circumstances in the most pleasant way possible. Help my words to reflect an understanding of Proverbs 16:24. ❧

FOOD FOR THOUGHT

1. Have you noticed that your children remember what you say long after you have forgotten? It is not a function of our diminished memory, but because of the power of our words. Make sure their memories are filled with positive words.
2. Memorize Proverbs 16:24. Keep this in your heart to prompt you to speak "pleasant words."
3. Consider saying less and listening more.

7 6

SPIRITUAL PRIORITIES

And it came to pass, that, as he was praying in a certain place,
when he ceased, one of his disciples said unto him,
Lord, teach us to pray, as John also taught his disciples.

LUKE 11:1

*A*ll of our children pray. They are all comfortable praying. We pray in public before a meal. We pray in our home. We have made a point of teaching our children to pray. What we need to do now is make sure we teach them *how* to pray. We need to teach them to pray for what matters in eternity as well as for temporal concerns. They need to learn to pray with specific thoughts in mind, not just whatever pops into their heads.

We keep hearing prayers for a nice day, that everything will go well, and similar requests. This is not wrong, but these requests have become a habit to the exclusion of praying for spiritual needs that matter more than having a nice day. Jesus taught His disciples to pray for God's will. He taught them to pray for daily provision, forgiveness of sins, forgiveness of others, and deliverance from evil. Such prayer has a spiritual foundation.

I am thinking of the types of prayers that I model for the children. Too often I end up praying about specific circumstances here on earth. I don't often enough model the spiritual emphasis that Jesus taught His disciples. In my private prayers I ask for God's will constantly. Ironically I seldom do this in my audible prayers with the children. I have been depriving them of a good example. I guess I didn't realize how important it was to teach them how to pray. If Jesus had to teach the disciples, this should be my cue to consider it important to teach my children.

Prayer has not been taken out of our homeschools. Prayer should be our foundation. We have unlimited opportunities each day to pray and to teach our children how to pray. There is power in prayer. If the thoughts of our children naturally turn toward matters here on earth, then we must teach them to pray with a heart for spiritual matters. The curriculum is so simple. Just model a heart for spiritual concerns in your audible prayers with your children. If this is a weak spot in your life, take the initiative now to strengthen it with your children. Homeschooling is such a good training ground for Mom.

Do your children pray only for matters here on earth, or do they have an eye on eternity?

PRAYER

Dear Jesus, You are such a good example to me of an effective teacher. Your own disciples needed instruction in how to pray. Of course my children do too. Help me to model prayer for them in a way that teaches them what is truly important in life. I desire for my own prayer life to be stronger. ❧

FOOD FOR THOUGHT

1. Are there prayer warriors in your church or on the radio who model fervent prayer? Learn from them.
2. Make teaching your children how to pray as important as other school subjects. It won't happen unless you make an effort.
3. Study the prayer model that Jesus gave the disciples in Luke 11:2-4. Teach this prayer to your children not as something to be memorized, but in terms of the content. Write out some prayers that follow this prayer pattern.

77

DO WHAT YOU CAN

The LORD will give strength unto his people;
the LORD will bless his people with peace.

PSALM 29:11

❧

I was very busy right before our annual state homeschool convention this year. I like to go through our bookshelves before the convention, so I can see what we have and determine what we need for the following year. Then I can purchase books at the convention and save money by not having to pay shipping. This year I did not have enough time to finish the task, but I started anyway. Although the list of books I needed was incomplete, I was just glad that I got some of it done.

I knew I could not finish the job when I started, but I started just the same. That is a change for me because I like to finish things. I can tense up if I have to leave too much unfinished. It is hard to be calm as a homeschooling mother because most tasks are in process and unfinished. You know how to do a good job, but there isn't enough time to do the job right; so you just get by and then feel bad about it. I don't feel peaceful when I am surrounded by unfinished business.

There is a better way. A lot of pressure can be eliminated when you focus on doing what you can do instead of looking at what you cannot do. I realized at the state convention that by buying most of my books at that time, I saved a lot of money on shipping. The few things I forgot could easily be ordered from a catalog. Calmness comes with an accurate assessment of your limitations. If you don't accept your limitations, you will be disappointed.

It is wise to seek God's direction daily so you know where to spend your time. Homeschooling is a lifestyle that dramatically affects your ability to finish anything completely the way you might like to. Acceptance of these conditions takes away the irritation that comes from feeling like you never get anything done. We get a lot done. The kingdom work we do in raising and training our children at home, while always in process, is certainly getting the job done for God. As we seek the Lord daily to determine priorities, we are blessed if we seek His strength. We can then rest in God's peace, knowing that we have done our best.

Are you calm even though it seems impossible to finish anything?

PRAYER

Father, thank You for teaching me so much about myself as I homeschool my children. I am grateful that I am more relaxed now and can overlook the unfinished tasks in my home in favor of the day's priorities. As I seek Your direction I see that eventually what matters does get finished. Help me to train my children to so rely on You that their schedules are incomplete if they have not prayed for Your priorities for each day. ❧

FOOD FOR THOUGHT

1. Are you a perfectionist? How does this affect your homeschooling?
2. Do you need to consider doing just an average job in some areas so you can focus on the most important needs in your family?
3. Identify your limitations and respect them.

78

STOP CRYING

My soul thirsteth for God, for the living God; when shall I come and appear before God? My tears have been my meat day and night, while they continually say unto me, Where is thy God?

PSALM 42:2-3

Are you ever so engulfed by your circumstances that you can't stop crying? You can think pleasant thoughts, but the tears still fall. You can decide that God allowed the circumstances and it will be all right, but the tears still flow. When you are overwhelmed, it can be difficult to calm down. Sometimes I become so emotionally distraught that I lose my appetite. During a recent trial I saw this verse in an entirely new light.

"My tears have been my meat day and night" accurately pictures what happens when I am so upset that I have no appetite. The tears consume me, and I don't feel like eating. The second part of the verse is the key to pulling out of my emotional fog. ". . . while they continually say unto me, Where is thy God?" If you think about uncontrollable crying in a spiritual way, you will find a solution. When the tears won't stop, it is time to drop everything and find God in the Bible and through prayer.

The Psalms offer much comfort for the hurting. It doesn't matter what the source of our pain is. These powerful chapters contain the comfort we are seeking. In trying circumstances, our inability to cope comes from the fact that we have lost hold of God. Our soul is longing for God, and when the Holy

Spirit fills that ache in us, we are better equipped to deal with our circumstances. Crying out to God in our prayers can bring the much needed answers to our difficulties.

Homeschooling is no easy endeavor. It may very well reduce you to tears. There may be a *lot* of tears. Parenting takes a stiff upper lip, and for a tender-hearted woman, this may seem impossible at times. It is not wrong to cry. It might be just the release you need to get through a challenging time. It might also be your wake-up call to draw nearer to God. He is always there, waiting for you to make the first move.

Have you cried out to God lately about anything?

PRAYER

Dear Jesus, help me to understand my emotions better. When I cry, help me to see beyond the tears to the deep need that I have right at that moment. Comfort me during the painful times. Thank You for being there for me when I take the initiative to get near to You. My circumstances have been a blessing because they have drawn me closer to You. ❧

FOOD FOR THOUGHT

1. Have you cried lately? Did your tears point you to the Lord?
2. Women cry. This is good. God gave us our tender emotional side, and we do well not to fight this. Allow your tears to draw you closer to the ultimate source of comfort, Jesus.
3. Teach your children to seek comfort in Christ when they cry. Particularly for boys, don't discourage their tears; rather, direct them to the Psalms for comfort. We do our sons a service by developing their emotional side instead of teaching them not to have one.

7 9

OBEDIENCE HAS BENEFITS

*My son, forget not my law; but let thine heart keep my
commandments: For length of days, and long life, and peace,
shall they add to thee.*

PROVERBS 3 : 1 - 2

❧

Parenting is very demanding. There it is. I have stated the obvious. What
is not always so clear is why parenting is so demanding. It is true there are
many areas that require our attention. But I find that one particular focus as
a parent takes away every bit of strength I have each day. It is teaching my children to listen to me and do what I tell them. Training children in obedience
is a formidable task.

Obedience training goes on every minute of every day. From their earliest years until they leave home, we are teaching our children about the relationship between authority and obedience. Lately our family has struggled
in the area of obedience. I find myself getting impatient with my children
and telling them to obey me because I am in charge when Dad is gone. This
is hardly proper motivation for obedience.

God shows us his way in Proverbs 3. Give your children a vision for the
benefits they will gain when they do it God's way. Proverbs 3:1-2 is powerful
as we understand each of the components. "My son, forget not my law" puts
the burden of remembering what to do on the child. It does not imply that
Dad or Mom needs to keep reminding them of the rules so they can obey. It

is here that we see God's desire for the child to take personal responsibility for knowing what is expected of him or her. ". . . but let thine heart keep my commandments" teaches them not to merely comply outwardly, but to take obedience seriously and to take what is required of them to heart.

The last part of the verse gives children a vision for the benefits of doing what I have just described. God tells us that "length of days, and long life, and peace" will be added to us when we obey. Peace is attractive. Who doesn't want peace? If peace comes from obedience, then what comes from disobedience? How much better to show our children what a sovereign God desires for them in the area of obedience rather than lording our position as parents in authority over them.

Have your children taken obedience to heart?

PRAYER

Heavenly Father, thank You for making Your desires for us so clear in Your Word. Help me teach my children what You want for them. My desire is that their motivation be that of a heart that wants to please You. Help me to be a good example of obedience to my children. When I fail, let humility be the dominant character quality in the situation. Obedience is key to everything else my children do. I pray that all of them will learn to respect authority and be obedient for Your glory. ❧

FOOD FOR THOUGHT

1. Have you trained your children to obey just because you tell them to? Expand your teaching to include the benefits that God says are a part of obedience.
2. Use Scripture often to direct your children. Their hearts must become tender toward what God wants at the earliest opportunity.
3. When children want to know why they must do something, tell them. Often they will be more motivated when they understand. Conversely, make sure they know they won't always know why.

THE ELECTRIC FENCE

The law of the wise is a fountain of life,
to depart from the snares of death.

PROVERBS 13:14

༄

We have a number of animals on our farm. Ponies, sheep, and goats are in our pasture. Their boundary is marked off by stakes with an electric fence. It only takes a brush up against the fence once or twice for the animals to realize they need to stay inside the fence. This is for their own protection, so they don't wander into the road and get lost or killed. They don't have sense enough to stay in the pasture without the fence. It is wise for us to keep them behind the electric fence.

The rules and standards that we have in our homes are the electric fences we provide for our children, who need boundaries for their own protection. They don't know what is appropriate for them without rules and standards. They would get lost. Two of our animals don't have to be behind the electric fence. Our collies, Callie and Brenna, have the run of the farm because they have been trained to stay on our property. Occasionally they wander and need to be called back. They come home quickly when called.

This is the goal I have for my children. As they are trained and as they show respect for our rules and standards, they will gain more freedom to make their own decisions. As long as they remain faithful to their training, they will have greater privileges. Occasionally we will have to call their attention to an area, and hopefully they will come running back quickly. It is wise for them to know the rules and standards and follow them. That provides protection for them.

Our children learn from the boundaries set by rules and standards, which make up the framework in which our children learn best. Learning to work within boundaries when young opens up great opportunities for them when they are older. Laws, boundaries, rules, and standards are a part of life. Respect for them is wise. Accepting them as a natural part of life brings much benefit to those who understand their purpose. They are not meant to be restrictive but instructive.

Does your family have rules and standards?

PRAYER

Dear Lord, thank You for the order that comes from having rules and standards in our home. I am glad that my children are learning to respect the boundaries that are set for them by the authority over them. They will be trained well for the workforce in this way. Help me to encourage them that rules are not meant to contain them but to instruct them. When they are faithful in following the rules, give us wisdom as we give them more freedom. ❧

FOOD FOR THOUGHT

1. What happens in the home when there are no rules or standards? Do you need to make any changes in your home?
2. How do you know what rules and standards produce the godly character you desire in your children? Ask God to show you specifically in His Word.
3. Be careful not to think that your rules and standards are "right" and everybody else's are wrong. Seek God continually to be sure what you are doing is pleasing to Him.

8 1

THE FLAT TIRE

He that diligently seeketh good procureth favor: but he that seeketh mischief, it shall come unto him.

PROVERBS 11:27

Josiah loves riding his bicycle. Even when the front tire went flat, he was undaunted. He knew where the bicycle pump was and tried to fill up the tire himself. He set out to do good. His brothers helped him when he had trouble. When the air leaked out again, he just kept riding on the flat tire. Jim got the tire fixed, and Josiah could hardly wait to get back on his bike. He asked me when the air was going to run out again. No doubt he was already planning on pumping up the tire if it should go flat.

At four years old Josiah learned a lot from this experience because we let him. In his heart he intended to do good and fix his own bike. He learned resourcefulness as he located the bicycle pump and asked for help. He learned tenacity when the air ran out again, but he kept on riding. He learned patience while he waited for his tire to be fixed.

It comes easily to us as parents to provide solutions for our children. It is more trouble to let children learn for themselves, but that is exactly what they need. They can be their own problem solvers. They need to develop character as they see a problem through to a solution. We don't need to always provide solutions for them. We can facilitate solutions by giving them instruction and allowing them time and resources (the bicycle pump) to learn for themselves. Even young children can learn on their own with supervision.

Children naturally get into mischief. How much better to provide resources for them to use to be creative problem solvers. If we train them to use tools or kitchen appliances properly, they will be more apt to seek these out to do good than if we restrict them from touching anything. My boys are eager to do work that involves motorized equipment. Anything that requires the tractor appeals to them. They stay out of trouble by using our resources to work and solve problems. With proper guidance their potential is greater than we can imagine, and their confidence soars with each problem solved. When we as parents do it all for them, we slow down the learning process. God lets us learn through experience. This is a good model for training children too.

What problems have you allowed your children to solve today?

PRAYER

Dear God, thank You for my husband's wisdom in allowing our children to use tools, computers, tractors, etc. to solve their own problems. They are a very creative group of young problem solvers as a result. They aren't afraid to try new things and have skills beyond their years. Help me to continue to facilitate problem solving rather than providing answers for them. Thank You for showing us what to do. ❧

FOOD FOR THOUGHT

1. Are your children capable of doing more to work through problems than you give them credit for? Let them use your resources (with instruction), and turn them loose. Allow them to fail.
2. Did your parents restrict you because they thought you would break something? How does this affect the way you are raising your children?
3. Give God the glory for the character building that comes when you facilitate rather than provide solutions for your children.

8 2

AVAILABLE TO HELP

But exhort one another daily, while it is called Today;
lest any of you be hardened through the deceitfulness of sin.

HEBREWS 3:13

❧

The first couple of years as a homeschool mom weren't too demanding. The children were young, and we were focused on beginning reading, basic math facts, and learning how to get along with each other. Some of our children still fit this description. But as the children grew and more babies joined our school, I had serious doubts about how I would juggle everything. Each day is a miracle of God's grace as I teach toddlers to teens in our home.

Our first homeschool support group had speakers at our monthly meetings. One night stands out in my mind. An older mother with high school children spoke to us. I can't remember the topic specifically, but I remember her teaching us that homeschooling did not have to be so complicated. She gave us practical tips and showed us how to apply them. That night she helped me free up my thinking and gave me a vision for making it all work. I was able to relax a little and realize that I really could homeschool successfully.

The temptation to keep to ourselves after we know what we are doing is dangerous. You may not feel like you need anyone, but there is probably someone who needs you. The Scripture calls us to "exhort one another daily." That means we need to do this often. The warning is there so that we are not hardened through "the deceitfulness of sin." We don't exhort other women if we don't put ourselves in situations to do this. If we become absorbed in our own life, we won't even be around other women who need encouragement.

Many homeschool moms find it nearly impossible to maintain even one close relationship with another mom. They invest themselves completely in homeschooling their children, while ignoring their own emotional needs. This may work for a while, but eventually burnout will most likely arrive in some form. Women *need* to exhort one another. They understand each other, and the veterans have wisdom that novices desperately need.

Are you a veteran homeschooler? Encourage the new moms. Are you a new homeschooler? Find a veteran to answer your questions.

PRAYER

Father, thank You for sending experienced homeschool moms across my path. They have helped me in many ways through the years. Help me to see opportunities to minister to new homeschool moms. Few people understand the homeschooling lifestyle, and supporting each other is so important. Help us to see the importance of relationships that build us up. Prompt me when my focus becomes inward and I fail to be a blessing to others. ❧

FOOD FOR THOUGHT

1. What percentage of the activities in your homeschool support group relate to children or field trips? Do you need to provide for fellowship between the mothers?
2. Take the time to invite other homeschool moms into your home for fellowship. As families visit together, this time affords your children a chance to learn to relate to others outside your family while under your supervision.
3. Do you have one good friend with whom you can share your joys and frustrations candidly? If not, seek a godly relationship with another homeschool mom.

8 3

MOTIVATED BY FAILURE

Being confident of this very thing, that he who hath begun
a good work in you will perform it until the day of Jesus Christ.

PHILIPPIANS 1:6

❧

Today I am living in the aftermath of yesterday. My intentions for the day were good. I had planned on cleaning our bookshelves and getting ready for the new curriculum I would be buying. It never happened. Instead I got caught up in a flurry of poor communication, hurtful words, and emptiness even after the final "I'm sorrys" had been said. The day finished with the discovery of disobedience in one of our older children that was particularly disturbing to me.

I fell short. When a simple request made of my husband was thrown back at me, I failed to remain calm. I kept talking throughout the day to try and communicate through the problem. I only made it worse. It ended finally, but it wasn't finished. I was misunderstood again, and now my sinful tongue had alienated my husband from me. And my older child turned out not to be as trustworthy as I had thought.

My heart was heavy as I attempted to sleep. How could I be so committed to being a godly wife and mother, yet have such poor results? How could I know the right things to do, yet do so many wrong things? I have never before felt a feeling of failure as deeply as I did last night. Emotionally painful, yesterday's deepest ache comes from realizing my own sin. My own inability to do God's will and be in a right relationship to God and to my own family is making me very sad. I feel like I am never going to get it right.

God knows this, and He knows me. He didn't begin the work in my life fifteen years ago to drop me on my face today. As much as it hurts, I know that God has allowed these circumstances into my life for my growth. If I give in to failure now, how will God complete His work in me? I feel like my efforts are of no use. I feel like a failure. I want to give up. But I can't. God is determined to continue the good work He began in me, and I have to let Him. It's the only right answer. But, oh, how it hurts!

Do you feel like a failure? Feel like quitting? Don't give up!

PRAYER

Dear God, thank You for motivating me through my failures. I can see where the flaws are and what needs to be changed. It is a slow process, but I can see that this is the way You teach me. Help me to learn what You want me to learn through each challenge You allow in my life. Help me to see past the pain and to the point of suffering. Teach me Your ways. I can see that mine just don't work. ✑

FOOD FOR THOUGHT

1. Have you done something lately that has caused grief and trouble? Did you know better? Confess it now to God and repent.
2. Ask yourself why God allows the trials of your life to come when they do. Learn everything you are supposed to learn from them or risk God's having to bring another trial to teach you the same thing.
3. Let failure motivate you to future success by allowing God to shape you.

84

FOCUS

So teach us to number our days,
that we may apply our hearts unto wisdom.

PSALM 90:12

❧

I'm not sure I could homeschool without a routine of some sort. During the winter our schedule is more rigid because I want us to get more done. The bulk of our "book school" is done during the winter months. I have a limited amount of time to finish a specified amount of material; so I aim to maximize our time. In the summer our learning is more relaxed, as is our schedule.

After twelve years of homeschooling I feel like I finally understand how to balance our days. That doesn't mean our days are always balanced. It means I can pretty well spot why we are out of balance and take steps to correct it. Much of the time our lack of balance ties into focus. We may focus too much in one area, or we focus in so many directions at once that we have a mess.

It helps to have deadlines. Deadlines in homeschooling are set by Mom and Dad. There is flexibility, but there must be deadlines. If we just keep working on books or projects with no targeted completion time, we often become distracted. If we have no deadlines, we fail to establish boundaries for our children. A family routine or schedule with regular waking and retiring times establishes a daily boundary. Regular mealtimes provide structure throughout the day.

There never really seems to be enough time. How important it is to redeem the time we do have each day! I have learned this principle well in the area of cleaning the house. I could work twenty-four hours a day on it and still never finish. Instead, I gather all of the children together, and we tidy up and clean the entire house in two hours. We do the most important jobs first, but it seems some jobs are never tackled. On another day we will make those a priority. This is all about priorities—understanding what is truly the most important and getting it done. This is wise.

How is your family routine doing?

PRAYER

Heavenly Father, thank You for enlightening me about how to integrate the needs of all family members into our routine. It challenges me to accommodate the ones who like a rigid schedule as well as those who don't want any schedule. Help me to set a pleasant tone in our home by structuring our routine as comfortably as possible. Give me the courage to schedule very demanding days when we need to accomplish much as well as to spend some unstructured, spontaneous time. My role as homeschool mom demands good organizational skills of me. Please help me as I seek to honor You in all that I do. ∞

FOOD FOR THOUGHT

1. Need help in establishing a workable routine for your own family? Order a tape of "Family Strategies to Energize Your Home" by Jackie Wellwood. (Order from Equipping the Family, 1-309-747-4400.)
2. Ask your children how they feel about your routine. Let them tell you what they would change to improve it. Dare to implement their suggestions.
3. What is your focus throughout the day? Are you trying to do too many things at once? It might help to write out your plans for the day with estimated times for each area of focus.

8 5

FOLLOWING GOD'S WILL

Though he were a Son, yet learned he obedience
by the things which he suffered.

HEBREWS 5:8

❧

A s a child I learned early on that if I obeyed my father, the outcome was pleasant. When my dad told me I could only ride my bike up to a certain street, I followed his directions. I was rewarded for my obedience with fewer restrictions in the future. I equated obedience with positive results. I developed a desire to follow directions wherever I was because I could see the relationship between doing this and having good things happen.

As a middle-aged woman, I find that obedience to God's will doesn't guarantee pleasant results. It might require pain. In the case of Jesus it resulted in death. For many years now Jim and I have believed the Bible's teaching that children are a reward from God. We do not make provision to block these blessings. Yet, soon after turning forty I miscarried a number of times in a short period of time. Losing twins, hemorrhaging, going into shock, visiting the hospital, and experiencing scary hormone imbalances hardly seem like positive results from following God's will. Or are they?

I sought answers to these losses and came up with little physically to explain them. Older women have a greater chance of miscarriage, but I seemed to be exceeding the statistics. Spiritually I began to see obedience to God's will in a new way. God's will isn't a situation with guaranteed outcomes. Sometimes obedience is painful, sometimes apparently unbearably so. But obedience is always profitable in the eyes of God.

I am seven weeks pregnant as I write today. Last week we saw a heart-beat on the ultrasound. Everything seems to be fine at this time. I can't explain why we have lost so many babies. I know that as we understand Scripture, we are in obedience to God's truth. Regardless of the outcome of this pregnancy, I know that we have honored the truth that God has revealed in His Word. We know it is His will for us to follow truth. My faith has grown through all of this pain. I am learning obedience by the things I am suffering. I believe God does reward us with children just as He says in the Bible. They are a blessing, and we are open to all He plans to give us. The process has become painful for us, but the pain does not make truth wrong.

Are you in obedience to God even when it hurts?

PRAYER

Father, I trust You with my life. I know that You love me and desire good for me. Sometimes Your will feels like harm. Help me see my situation from Your point of view. Show me the errors in my ways so that I might be pleasing to You. Be with me in the next few weeks as my faith is tested with this pregnancy. Thank You for giving me the opportunity to serve You. ❧

FOOD FOR THOUGHT

1. Is there an area in your life where you are refusing to follow God's will because it is too painful? Repent and correct this now.
2. What is a proper response to suffering? Have you let it develop patience in your life?
3. Memorize Hebrews 5:8. Let this verse help you see the benefits of suffering.

86

HELP ME, LORD

I cried to thee, O LORD;
and unto the LORD I made supplication.

PSALM 30:8

❧

I have been handicapped by pride for most of my life. Ouch, that hurt! I don't even like to think about this, let alone tell you about it. Much of this handicap has been evidenced by my failure to ask for help. Even as a child I tended toward independence. As I grew toward adulthood I became convinced that if I worked hard enough and smart enough I could do anything.

Then I began homeschooling. Gradually I started to wonder if I could ever do enough or be enough to make homeschooling work. I tried it in my own power for a long time. I became impatient and angry as the lifestyle began to consume me. Instead of thriving, I was merely surviving. Knowing full well I had a sovereign God who oversees all of this, I continued to work harder myself. I read more how-to books, attended conventions, and did anything else I could think of to help myself. I kept streamlining and learning and was able to be successful in this manner for a while.

Until I reached the point where I could not juggle it all anymore, I neglected my most precious resource. I did not consciously exclude God. It just didn't occur to me to ask for much. I still thought what happened in my life was due to something I had either done or not done. I did not understand the mighty hand of God. I certainly did not comprehend that God can do anything. I clearly did not believe He would. It never occurred to me that He wanted to help me.

Then, desperate for a miracle, I cried out for help. Me, the one who never asked for help, cried out to God for help! I couldn't get away with trying to do it in my own power anymore. Completely exhausted, burned-out, and ready to quit, I asked God for help. Guess what He did? He helped me—a lot! I should have done this before resentments and irritations turned to anger. I should have thrown my hands up at the beginning of homeschooling and cried out for help. He doesn't want us to do this alone. He is there. He wants to help you. All you have to do is ask.

Has He heard your cry yet?

PRAYER

Dear Lord, thank You for helping me. Forgive me for trying to do myself what only can be done with Your help. Without You I am nothing. Whatever talents and abilities I have are from You. Help me to please You each day by directing my steps. Thank You that I am more relaxed and calmer in my home by Your grace. I could not do it without You. ❦

FOOD FOR THOUGHT

1. Before the irritations of the day overcome you, do you have a plan to keep from getting angry? Can you get away by yourself to pray for a few minutes?
2. Do you feel comfortable asking for help?
3. Be specific when you tell your husband what you need. For example, if you need help with the housework, time to yourself, or a hug, tell him exactly what it is, so he will know how to help you.

How Am I Motivated?

For I know that in me (that is, in my flesh) dwelleth no good thing:
for to will is present with me; but how to perform
that which is good I find not.

ROMANS 7:18

It was 6:15 A.M. on a Saturday morning when four-year-old Josiah banged on our bedroom door. He was already dressed and ready to start his day. He had an agenda. The day before, I had purchased new colored pencils, and he wanted to make a picture with them. The night before, he had trouble falling asleep because he was thinking about his new pencils. He wanted to be creative!

Josiah was motivated. It was as though nothing could hold him back. His enthusiasm was contagious. I got up and got him started on his coloring project. When was the last time I had so much enthusiasm? What would motivate me? Would it be a new dishwasher? A dress? Would time alone to read and think motivate me? What did I need?

We already know that we need to motivate our children. But do you realize that you need to know what motivates *you*? Let your husband be creative and do something out of the ordinary to motivate you. Maybe he can see a need in your life that you are missing. Jim has selected a larger breed pony to purchase, so I can ride along with one of our children riding on our smaller pony, Ginger. My first reaction was cautious because this is a financial stretch

I am not sure is timely. After sharing my concerns, Jim was still convinced this would be a good idea.

I understand why he is doing this. He knows I have been working too hard and need to have some fun. He believes the pony would be good for me. I have a tendency to work too much, and the pony would be a totally new interest that would be just for fun. This could be what I need in order to be revived after dealing with burnout for over a year. A burned-out mother is hardly a motivation to her children. I need something to bring back my enthusiasm. We all need to keep motivated. What accomplishes this will vary, but we need to find something to keep us going. We need to let others bless us with some fun. Most of us probably need to lighten up a bit and enjoy the journey.

What keeps you motivated?

PRAYER

Heavenly Father, I am grateful that my husband is thoughtful of me. While the purchase of this pony seems to be out of our reach, if it is supposed to be, it will work out. Thank You for showing me that fun is a part of our homeschool. Not only fun for the children, but fun for Mom too. Help me again with balance in our home. Let it be a happy place that all of our family enjoys. ❧

FOOD FOR THOUGHT

1. Do you provide for some fun activities or hobbies that are just for you?
2. Do you have any signs of burnout? Are you ready to give up? Give yourself a break instead, and pick out something fun that motivates you.
3. Ask your husband if he has any suggestions for you. You may be pleasantly surprised.

8 8

GOD HEALS THE WOUNDS

He healeth the broken in heart, and bindeth up their wounds.

PSALM 147:3

☙

*I*t is amazing to me how much our loved ones can hurt us at times. They don't mean to, but human relationships are delicate. We too wound others easily when we don't even know it. An ill word spoken at the wrong time hurts deeply. As women, we feel emotional pain acutely. Harshness and insensitivity slice through us like a knife. No matter how good a relationship is, there will be some tough times.

When I am brokenhearted, I look for someone to console me. I usually look to my husband for this comfort. If it is Jim who has broken my heart, then the situation is more difficult. I feel frustrated and alone because it feels like my closest friend has become my archenemy. This is not at all true, but it still feels that way. When we put our hope in other people, we are easily disappointed.

During one particular difficulty, it seemed there was nobody to help me. I felt the Lord drawing me nearer to Himself in my despair. I know that I am supposed to "lean on the Lord," but never before did I see this as enough. I thought if I could just find one person to show me what to do in my situation, then my pain would subside and I would be doing better. The trouble is, it isn't other people who heal our pain.

If God heals the broken heart and binds the wounds, then it must be God to whom we turn in our hour of need. It is God's grace that enables us to bear up under our circumstances. It is God's power that can bring about a change in the circumstances. It is God's wisdom that we need to see us through our difficulty.

Whom are you depending on?

PRAYER

Dear Jesus, I am glad that You are there for me. Lately it seems that You have allowed more and more circumstances into my life that other people can't really help me with. I believe this is no accident. My tendency to look for flesh and blood to talk to has kept me from seeking You with my whole heart. I am near to You now and appreciate the trials that have come to draw me to You. You are so good to me. Forgive me for doubting Your role in my circumstances. I see that the challenges are placed before me for my training in righteousness, and how I respond to them is important. It is my desire to accept whatever You have for me each day. ❧

FOOD FOR THOUGHT

1. Do you have a special person whom you seek for help when the tough times come? Do you consult this person before or after consulting God?
2. How do you view your circumstances? Are the trials a nuisance, or are they designed to draw you closer to God? How do you respond to the trials?
3. Think of the time in your life that you felt the closest to God. Was it during a time of crisis? How can you be sure that you are close to God daily?

8 9

GOD IS THE LEADER

Thus saith the LORD, thy Redeemer, the Holy One of Israel;
I am the LORD thy God which teacheth thee to profit,
who leadeth by the way that thou shouldest go.

ISAIAH 48:17

I have noticed large families with quiet, well-behaved children. I have been told that our children are well-behaved, and for the most part I believe this to be true. I do not recall, however, anyone ever complimenting me on how quiet my children are. There is good reason for this. They are loud! Oh, we do fairly well in public, but at home where their personalities flourish, it is quite noisy.

One day Jim and I were discussing our children. We were contemplating why there isn't a calm and quiet one in the bunch. What he told me made me cringe. He said that the reason our children butt heads so often is because they are all trying to be leaders. My neighbor recently observed the same thing. Now, how do you raise all leaders without any followers? I immediately thought of many reasons why this discovery would make my job more difficult.

If they are all trying to lead, then I have to work extra hard to make sure they are relating well to each other. They need to consider each other's needs and respect their parents' authority over them. They need to learn their place in the family. There is more. Wouldn't it be easier if we had a few passive children who would just follow? It might, but what a blessing to have children who are on fire.

As part of their preparation for leadership, we are actively teaching each one of them to follow. We require young children to follow the responsible direction of older children. Sometimes younger children will have responsibility for something, and older children will need to respect them. All of the children are learning to follow (honor) their father by obeying him. All of the children are taught that God is the One who directs us and that to be in His will is the best place to be. Good leaders need to know how to follow first. As they follow God's leadership (through parents), they will learn where God wants them to be.

Are you raising leaders?

PRAYER

Dear Lord, I need help. I don't know how to train a house full of leaders. They are strong and persistent, which creates conflicts as they are learning to relate properly to one another. Help me to see the character qualities that each one of them needs to develop. Help me to be excited by their enthusiasm instead of letting it overwhelm me. Please let me be a good example to them as an authority in their lives. I want them to know that You are their ultimate authority and their example of good leadership. ❧

FOOD FOR THOUGHT

1. How do your children respond to authority? Do they like to be in charge?
2. Does your oldest child have the tendency to take over when given responsibility in the home? This is normal for firstborns, who need a little extra training in this area.
3. Make a special effort to require your "natural born leaders" to learn how to follow.

90

THERE IS HOPE

*And let us consider one another to provoke unto love and
to good works: Not forsaking the assembling of ourselves together,
as the manner of some is; but exhorting one another: and
so much the more, as ye see the day approaching.*

HEBREWS 10:24-25

I need encouragement as a homeschool mom. The hours are long, and the requirements are many. Some days are great, but there are other times I really benefit from the kind words of another who understands. Those who don't homeschool have a difficult time relating to my lifestyle. It helps to have fellowship with other moms who face similar challenges. Recently I saw a way of providing for this need on a regular basis.

I like to have women visit my home once a month. That gives my daughters an opportunity to learn hospitality. We are now inviting homeschool moms to our home on a monthly basis for the sole purpose of building relationships. It is natural for us to exhort one another as we are gathered together. Our programs each month reflect the desire to encourage love and good works. This is a night designed specifically for homeschool moms for their benefit.

We have named our little gathering HOPE (Homeschoolers Offering Practical Encouragement). Hope is what we often lack when our patience is worn thin. Hope is what we lack when we see little fruit for our efforts. Hope is what we need when we aren't sure whether we can keep doing so much work. Hope is what we need to pursue such a calling as homeschooling.

We make time for field trips, spelling bees, and enrichment programs. We keep our ears open for opportunities for our children. A superior opportunity for the children is for Mom to have some time with other women who are being encouraged to love and to do good things. When Mom comes home with her batteries charged, she is better able to be the best homeschool mom she can be.

Do you have fellowship with other women in a context in which you exhort one another?

PRAYER

Father, I appreciate the opportunity that I have to homeschool my children. Thank You for showing me the importance of encouraging other women. I pray that you will bless our HOPE meetings and that many will be encouraged. Help us to grow in character as we learn about Your desires for each one of us. Bless other women who seek to meet together to exhort each other as homeschool moms. Grant us wisdom as we minister to each other. Open our hearts to the needs of others outside our family. ❧

FOOD FOR THOUGHT

1. Consider getting together with another homeschool mother or two to have a devotional time using this book or my earlier book *101 Devotions for Homeschool Moms*. Use the devotions as a springboard for discussion. Pray for each other regarding specific areas of need.
2. Do you know of any homeschool moms in need of encouragement? Take on a ministry of encouragement by creatively looking for ways to meet these needs. Don't overlook the easier helps such as sharing your curriculum catalogs with a new homeschool mom.
3. As you purpose to encourage other women, notice that many of your own needs will be met through your acts of service for others.

9 1

DO THEY FEEL LOVED?

This is my commandment,
That ye love one another, as I have loved you.

JOHN 15:12

❧

I was driving on the interstate when a red Porsche caught my eye. On the license plate I saw the words, "Lov Me." I began thinking about what the young man driving the car had in mind when he requested that license plate. It struck me as a pleading request for love. Somehow it seemed that he didn't feel loved and was crying out for it. How did this happen?

My thoughts turned to my own children, and I wondered if each one of them feels loved. It is possible to be busy working in the home throughout the day and not ever show love to your children. It is possible to homeschool your children in such a way that they don't feel loved. There is a difference between knowing in your heart that you love your children and expressing it to them in a way that they will understand.

Mother's Day has recently passed, and judging by the cards I received I can tell my children feel loved. I don't show my love to each of them the same way. My older girls feel loved when I spend time listening to them, take them shopping, or get them a special treat. Offering to relieve them from washing or drying dishes speaks to their hearts also.

My boys feel loved when I spend time in their world. Arm wrestling (so far I can still beat them), pulling the sled with the snowmobile, cross-country skiing, and riding the four-wheeler are all ways I connect with them. The younger girls just like to be with me. The common denominator is time and talk. They don't feel loved because our school days run perfectly. They don't feel loved because of all of the laundry and meals that I facilitate. They feel loved because I spend time with them and we talk. Sometimes we talk a lot. Sometimes there just isn't enough time.

Do your children feel loved?

PRAYER

Dear Lord, thank You for the tremendous amount of time that I have each day with my children. I don't know how I would even know them if they were away from the home each day. Thank You for blessing me with talkative children. Every single one of them likes to share what he or she is thinking. Help me to keep the lines of communication open at night when I have already been talking with them for over ten hours in the day. I sense a great bonding that takes place when we take time to talk. Keep me sensitive to their needs and how I can meet them. Alert me to anyone in our family who doesn't feel loved. ❧

FOOD FOR THOUGHT

1. Are you more task-oriented or relationship-oriented? If you focus on tasks, make sure you spend enough time talking with your children throughout the day.
2. Ask each of your children what makes him or her feel loved. Answers will probably be different for each child. Write down their answers, so you can meet their love needs better.
3. What makes you feel loved? Ask your husband if it would be okay if you told him as part of this exercise. Find out what makes him feel loved too, and write this on your list.

A WAY TO HELP

*For even the Son of man came not to be ministered unto,
but to minister, and to give his life a ransom for many.*

MARK 10:45

༄

As a new homeschooler I could see that it would be challenging to try to fit into the structure of the church. We kept our children with us during the service. I did not put my babies in the nursery. We decided to focus on family activities rather than "one child goes here and another goes there" type of choices. That has worked well for us, but trying to fit into traditional church structure has been a struggle.

When we moved to our farm, we had the opportunity to attend a church where it is common to homeschool, have large families, have all of our children in the worship service with us, and participate in activities as a family. This family-friendly church structure has been easier to fit into, but we are challenged because the church is located quite a distance from our farm. Jim's work schedule and the distance we live from church precludes many commitments I could make. Sometimes I wonder if I will ever feel like I am connected to the women at church.

Feeling frustrated by all of this, one day I decided that I would make a point of noticing which women at church seemed to be troubled and take time to talk with them. A godly older woman encouraged me that this is an important ministry. Though I had been diligently looking for a way to fit into the existing structure of our church, I had missed God's will for me in my own particular circumstances.

In our unique situation, God had a special job for me. I could still minister to others who were in need informally. I don't just come to church to hear excellent preaching; I come to encourage other women whenever I can. When I pray before I go to church that God would show me who needs a smile, I can be assured that He will direct me. God's will for me fits my circumstances perfectly as I seek to bless others at church as well as to be fed myself.

How do you fit into your church?

PRAYER

Dear Jesus, there are so many hurting people around us. Help me to be a blessing to those women whom I see each week at church. Some days I don't feel like reaching out. On those days help me to encourage others and so be lifted out of my own troubles in the process. Thank You for the many women I have had the privilege to meet. So many of them have left me with kind words that were a balm to my soul. Let me do the same. ❧

FOOD FOR THOUGHT

1. Do you see any needs in your church that are not being met? Can you meet any of these informally through talking with women or by showing hospitality? These can be arranged to fit around your schedule.
2. Do you have church responsibilities that put a burden on your family because the commitment does not fit well with homeschooling? Is there any way to redesign what you are doing so it would be better for your family? A proper appeal to the pastor can be very positive.
3. Are your family commitments and church commitments out of balance? Do you need to reevaluate what you are doing in terms of your family goals? Could you take on a new responsibility that would include your children in service?

9 3

$\mathcal{F}\mathcal{A}\mathcal{M}\mathcal{I}\mathcal{L}\mathcal{Y}$ $\mathcal{D}\mathcal{E}\mathcal{V}\mathcal{O}\mathcal{T}\mathcal{I}\mathcal{O}\mathcal{N}\mathcal{S}$

Study to show thyself approved unto God, a workman that needeth not to be ashamed, rightly dividing the word of truth.

2 TIMOTHY 2:15

I enjoy our family devotions. Due to the challenges of my husband's fire-fighter's work schedule, we have found that the most consistent time for our family to sit down together is right after lunch at 1:00. Sometimes all of the children are attentive, and I walk away feeling like we really learned something. Other times it seems almost impossible for anyone to focus on God's Word.

I wish the following description only happened once, but it happens more frequently than that. My children are young (ages three to fifteen), and the little ones are very creative at finding ways to make their older siblings laugh. Sitting down together at midday right after a meal makes it more difficult for them to settle down. I remember one day when we were really having trouble.

Several children were burping, and others were struggling with the challenges that come when your lunch includes refried beans. Everyone was distracted. Jim and I just looked at each other and continued to try to settle our family down. After a child had to go to the bathroom, my husband remarked, "With seven children we need seven corners." Some days separating them from each other is the best method. Other days we have to rearrange which children are sitting next to each other. At the end of our devotions we gather for prayer on the stairs in our living room. In the middle of our prayer time, a bird hit our window, and the distractions began all over again.

It sounds like our family devotions are a disaster. They aren't; this is just real life. Beyond hearing God's Word read, we are bonding as a family. Children are learning to sit next to each other without elbowing the other person. The children are learning to sit quietly and listen when one of them asks a question. This is a process that over time will produce a more "refined" family devotional time. Right now, since so many of our children are young, we are establishing a habit of family devotions. We are training for appropriate behavior. We are trying to be patient with the process.

What is your family learning during family devotions?

PRAYER

Dear God, thank You for a husband who leads our family devotions. Thank You for children who want to learn. Help us to be patient with the many lessons they are learning about sitting still, keeping quiet, and being attentive. I pray that Your Word would make a difference in their lives even during these times of training. I desire that the older ones would set good examples for the younger ones. Help us to faithfully set aside a time daily for family devotions. Thank You for directing our family through the reading of Your Word. ❧

FOOD FOR THOUGHT

1. Have you made provision for a regular time of family devotions? This is an important priority to establish for each day.
2. For young children, learning to sit quietly and listen is an important part of family devotions. Teaching them to do this yields great benefits in other situations outside the home.
3. Consider challenging your older children with questions that may require research, and have them report back at the next family devotional time.

9 4

DON'T MAJOR ON MINORS

But why dost thou judge thy brother?
Or why dost thou set at nought thy brother?
for we shall all stand before the judgment seat or Christ.

ROMANS 14:10

*H*omeschoolers tend to be different. Our worldview and the way we approach many issues can be radically different from those around us. It can be a challenge to fit in with others who are so unlike us. Much of the time it seems that we are misunderstood. Graciously loving others is the example Christ has given us to get along in this world. This is true for homeschoolers relating to other homeschoolers too.

How can it be that we have trouble with our own differences as homeschoolers? Why do we have so many opinions about issues that are minor? Contrary to popular misconception we do not all wear denim jumpers, bake our own bread, sew our own clothes, have large families and long hair, and wear no makeup. That's wonderful. We are a diverse group of families committed to educating our children at home. We aren't all supposed to look exactly like each other.

When I began homeschooling I had been a Christian for three short years. As I was growing in the Lord, I was learning about modest clothing. Both Jim and I reached a point where the Lord convicted us that I should wear dresses. Except for certain situations on our farm and walking on our treadmill, I mostly wear dresses, jumpers, skirts, and culottes. My husband likes this, and so do I. Some of you might feel that I should never wear pants, and others of you can't figure out why I wear dresses. That's okay.

What my husband thinks governs what I do. The trouble we have as homeschoolers is that we think we should all be the same. When our standards differ, we can be judgmental of those whose standards are not like our own. This should not be. Each individual family must account for their choices to the Lord, and wives are held accountable to their husbands, not to the opinions of other women. Women must not condemn each other for the standards in each of their homes. Christ's example of loving others should be our guide as we relate to other homeschooling families.

Do you evaluate other families based on their standards?

PRAYER

Heavenly Father, this is a sensitive area. I have been wounded by homeschoolers who have an air about them of being better than our family because of what they perceive to be higher standards in their family. I don't want to be this way. Please remove me from the presence of those who pick at the nonessentials without loving others. Strengthen us as homeschoolers to be known for our love, not our condemnation of one another. Our testimony as Christians is at stake if we look down on those who are not just like us. This was not the way of Jesus. ❧

FOOD FOR THOUGHT

1. What are the essentials in the Christian life? Is it the condition of the heart, or is it the externals?
2. How can we share what we know about areas such as modest clothing and bread making without alienating others? Do we make other people feel inferior because they don't know what we do? Be careful.
3. Why do we have music and dress standards? What is their purpose in our families?

ΝΟΤ ΜΥ WILL

And he went a little further, and fell on his face, and prayed, saying,
O my Father, if it be possible, let this cup pass from me:
nevertheless not as I will, but as thou wilt.

MATTHEW 26:39

⌇

After I spoke at a homeschool convention, a woman came to our book table with many questions. She was having many problems and wasn't sure how to solve them. I listened as she described her situation, and I offered suggestions where appropriate. Resistant to some of what I had said, she went on talking for some time. Finally she related something that made me wonder if her problems didn't somehow relate to this new information.

She told me that she had prayed and fasted so that she would not have to homeschool. Now after all efforts to avoid homeschooling had failed, she found herself homeschooling her son, who had been home from private school for eight weeks. Since she was determined to follow "her plan" even though she wasn't getting results, my recommendations fell on deaf ears. I wondered how long homeschooling could last in circumstances like these.

If it wasn't God's will for me to homeschool, I wouldn't want to do it. I want to be in God's will—always. I have my ideas and plans that I share with God, and then at the end I add on, "if this is Your will for me." What I want may not match up with God's plan. Christ is the perfect example. He really did not want to go through the ordeal that lay ahead of Him at the cross.

He asked God if it were possible to skip it, but then finished by saying that He wanted God's will.

Deciding to homeschool is a major life decision. It should be made in accordance with God's will. It is not a fallback position when every other avenue fails. Homeschooling is not for everyone. Prayerful consideration of many aspects is crucial to making the right decision. Once you have established that homeschooling is God's will for your family, then you can embrace it wholeheartedly, knowing God is with you in the endeavor.

Is homeschooling just something that sounds good, or is it God's will for your family?

PRAYER

Dear God, what a demanding calling it is to homeschool! Thank You for making Your will clear to us. Knowing that this is what You want for our family helps me get through the tough times. Help me to set aside my own desires and preferences when they go against Your will for me. Make my paths straight as I seek to honor You in all that I do. Help me to be sensitive to others when they are considering homeschooling. While I can share the benefits of homeschooling with them, they need to be sure that it is Your will for their family. ❧

FOOD FOR THOUGHT

1. Why have you decided to homeschool? What keeps you homeschooling?
2. How does knowing something is God's will, not your own, help you when the going gets tough? If homeschooling is simply your own idea, what do you do on a bad day when you change your mind?
3. Praise God for the special opportunity to educate your children in your home. Make a list of all the advantages of homeschooling.

9 6

TREAT THEM RIGHT

*Because sentence against an evil work is not executed speedily,
therefore the heart of the sons of men is fully set in them to do evil.*

ECCLESIASTES 8:11

The older girls (ages twelve and fourteen) were making negative comments
to the boys (ages eight and ten) during lunch one day. It was the kind of talk
that many accept as normal these days, although it does not honor God. In a
thoughtless moment I told the boys to just ignore the girls when they talked
that way. Eight-year-old Jonathan remarked, "I wish I could take my ears off
like Mr. Potato Head." I laughed, realizing this would easily solve the problem
the boys were having with their sisters.

Or would it? What was I doing? I suddenly realized that I was encouraging my sons to ignore their future wives when they said something my
sons did not want to hear. I was teaching my boys to ignore their future
wives when they brought up a problem that needed to be heard. I was teaching my daughters to talk inappropriately to their future husbands. By not
addressing the girls' negative talk, I was implying to them that they could
talk in whatever manner they wished. If I let this type of behavior continue,
it would become a habit that wouldn't be so easy to break. I needed to change
my approach to the problem.

I must train the girls how to relate properly to the boys. I must teach
the boys to be attentive to the girls. This is not easy, but it is necessary if my

children are going to learn how to communicate well. Good communication skills are learned. We have a perfect environment to teach communication. Learning to relate properly to siblings is excellent training. Brothers and sisters treating each other appropriately sets the stage for husbands and wives who do the same.

Sometimes the banter back and forth between the girls and the boys can be funny. The bickering is over inconsequential things most of the time. But we can't minimize this. We can't laugh. We must address it promptly and not allow it to continue. This takes diligence on our part, but if we fail to deal with inappropriate dialogue quickly, their hearts are "fully set in them to do evil."

How do your children talk to each other?

PRAYER

Father, I am sorry that I haven't been a very good example of how to relate to my husband properly. Thank You for guiding and teaching me how to improve in this area. Let me be a good model for communication that edifies and encourages. Make me sensitive to wrong attitudes in the children that are reflected in the way they talk to each other. Remind me to praise appropriate communication often. This is so important, and I feel inadequate to teach this effectively. ❧

FOOD FOR THOUGHT

1. Do you actively teach your children how to treat each other in a God-honoring way? Role-playing proper conflict resolution can give them ideas on how to handle their problems more effectively the next time.
2. Humble yourself when you do not talk to family members the way you should. Don't give your children the impression that your poor role model is okay for them to follow.
3. Cry out to God for daily help in training sons and daughters to relate well to each other.

9 7

ƒAMILY INƒLUENCE

He that walketh with wise men shall be wise,
but a companion of fools shall be destroyed.

PROVERBS 13:20

I had the privilege of participating in the interview process of a major Christian TV station that was selecting a cohostess for a new women's talk show. They needed someone to interview during their audition. My first book, *The Busy Mom's Guide to Simple Living*, had just been released, and it was decided that I should be the person the cohostess hopefuls would interview.

It was an exciting experience for me, and I learned a lot. What I recall most vividly is the question about $100 Nike athletic shoes. The hostess of the program kept asking me during each interview what I did when my children came home and wanted $100 Nike shoes like their friends. I graciously answered the question differently from what she was expecting. I explained that we don't have that problem because their clothing choices are not directed by their peers.

In each interview this same question was asked, as if the cohostess was thinking that somehow my answer would change. Those women could not understand that it would be possible for our children not to be peer-focused in their clothing selections. It occurred to me that students in public and private schools are heavily influenced by the peers with whom they spend many long hours a day while in school. My children are learning in my home, and we as parents guide them regarding acceptable clothing. Now, my boys do wear Nikes—they are purchased in "like new" condition for a few dollars at garage sales.

The main sphere of influence for homeschooled children should be their family. Most of their time is spent together in the home. The home is the influence that dominates their life. Clothing that my children wear is acceptable to Jim and me, even though some of their selections might not be what we would wear ourselves. We don't have battles over clothes that they are demanding because someone else has them. That is a nonissue in our home. More importantly, we are teaching them to dress in a way that honors God, looks good on them, and takes into account their personal preferences.

Do parents or peers have the greatest influence in your home?

PRAYER

Lord, what a blessing it is to eliminate some of the typical problems faced by youth today simply by choosing to homeschool. I am grateful that our family is the dominant influence in the lives of our children. Help us to be aware of peer influence when it begins to undermine what we are doing in our family. I am thankful that it is our influence they receive each school day. I am blessed by the fruit that I am seeing in my children. ❧

FOOD FOR THOUGHT

1. Are peer relationships undermining the authority God has given you over your children? Take steps to reduce or eliminate peer influences until your family stabilizes.
2. Have the courage to reject cultural pressures to dress in trendy fashions, choosing to honor God by your choices. Look for quality clothing in resale shops and garage sales.
3. Refuse to let clothing be a dominant topic, preferring more important considerations such as character.

COMMUNICATION 101

Unto the woman he said, I will greatly multiply thy sorrow and
thy conception; in sorrow thou shalt bring forth children;
and thy desire shall be to thy husband, and he shall rule over thee.

GENESIS 3:16

It is no surprise that men and women have difficulty communicating with each other. Whole books have been written about how differently men and women communicate. It is a struggle. It takes work—hard work. It requires commitment to keep trying when all lines of communication are down.

What surprises me is that after knowing my husband for twenty-five years, we still don't communicate very well at times. In the five years since my first book was published, I have received many calls and letters from women who "feel like they know me." They like the fact that I am real. If so many strangers can understand me, why doesn't my closest friend?

The answer lies in the gender. Men have difficulty understanding women. One result of the Fall in the Garden of Eden was that God said our husbands "shall rule over" us. In filling this role, the husband must take time to understand his wife, so he can be a better guide for her. Homeschool moms are so often misunderstood by neighbors, their family, and their church that to be misunderstood by their own husbands becomes particularly painful.

We can help our husbands be successful. Men are concrete thinkers. We need to talk to them concretely because that is the way they will best understand us. Simplifying what we are trying to say helps to minimize mis-understanding. Writing down our thoughts may clarify what we are trying to convey. We must be careful to approach them with our concerns at a time that is good for them. Never (and I mean *never*) take on a difficult subject just before bed unless both of you are committed to staying awake until the problem is resolved. Communication with our husbands is critical to the harmony that God desires for our families.

How well are you and your husband communicating?

PRAYER

Dear Lord, I confess to You that I haven't worked hard enough at understanding my husband because I was focused on being understood myself. Help me to talk with my husband in such a way that he can understand me. Help me to be less emo-tional, so he can hear my words better. As much as women seem to get to know me easily, I see that I need to work harder at my relationship with Jim. Thank You that we have made as much progress as we have. I look forward to learning more from You in this area. ❧

FOOD FOR THOUGHT

1. Do you have regular times of dialogue with your husband about any con-cerns you have about the children, the home, or anything else? Guard these times from interruptions.
2. If your husband does not understand you, try new techniques to explain what you mean to him. Try word pictures built around a favorite hobby of his such as golfing or fishing.
3. Keep a sweet spirit about you when your husband is ruling over you bet-ter than he is relating to you. Select a good time to make an appeal when it is necessary. Don't just be quiet, but learn to reverence your husband by the words you choose and the tone of voice you use to say them.

fellowship with families

Distributing to the necessity of saints; given to hospitality.

ROMANS 12:13

❧

*I*n our day there seems to be a redefining of the word *hospitality*. Dining in a restaurant with another family and opening your home to them are viewed as being the same thing. While dining in restaurants is fine, I do not believe it replaces what Paul refers to as being "given to hospitality" in the book of Romans.

It is easy to just view our homes as a place to live for our own family. They are that, but our homes are also much more than that. Our homes can be a place of blessing to others who visit with us over a meal. Having people into our homes is an investment as we tidy up, prepare the meal, serve it, and clean up. We offer something of ourselves in the process. It tells our guests that they are important to us since we took the trouble to prepare for them.

I have less and less time to visit with my friends over the telephone. Fellowship that we have when families come over is better and has greater depth than telephone calls that are frequently interrupted by the minute-to-minute needs of the family. In our home husbands and children get to fellowship too, and I can talk to my friend more intimately. As we invite others to our home, we allow them to enjoy what God has given to us. On our farm we have a pony that the children can ride. What a blessing it is to be able to share this with other families who do not have a pony.

Having people over for a meal isn't about perfectly decorated or spotlessly clean houses. It is not about gourmet meals either. It is about generously serving others who come to visit. Some of the best fellowship our family has ever experienced has been when entire families came to our home for a meal. My husband benefits from time to get to know other godly men, something that does not happen in his workplace. My children thrive when they play as a family with other families where older children help younger ones and all ages can be friendly with each other. Committing to be a hospitable family has many pleasures that become yours as you serve others.

When was the last time you had a family over for a meal?

PRAYER

Dear Lord, thank You for showing me the importance of opening my home to others. You have graciously provided a large home that makes this possible with larger families. I remember the blessings that came when we lived in smaller homes and made the best of what we had. Thank You for the enthusiasm my daughters have for hospitality. Show us whom You would like us to invite over next. ❧

FOOD FOR THOUGHT

1. Do you worry about how your house looks so much that it paralyzes you when you think about inviting people into your home? Visit someone else's home that has the "lived in" look. Notice that it didn't affect your fellowship negatively.
2. Design your living standard to be slightly below your entertaining standard so that getting ready for guests is fairly easy.
3. Keep a list of families you would like to invite over. Invite a family for a meal every month or two.

100

THE FLOWERS DIED

He becometh poor that dealeth with a slack hand:
but the hand of the diligent maketh rich.

PROVERBS 10:4

❧

I like flowers. I like to grow flowers that we can cut and put in bouquets for our table. I don't know too much about flowers, and my efforts have had average results. In the future I would like to do more with flowers around our house, but for now I usually plant wave petunias. I have some pots on my porch, and they are beautiful as the wave petunias fill out over the summer. This year I noticed that six-year-old Joanna was interested in flowers; so I asked her to water them each day.

We planted some wave petunias in an old stock pot and put them on an old table under a tree. It looked quaint, and I liked it. About a week ago I walked by and noticed that the flowers has shriveled up and died. The other petunias on the porch were fine, and I think that the dead ones hadn't been watered. They flourished for a while but then did not thrive as they were left unattended for too long. I was surprised at how quickly their condition deteriorated.

What a parallel these dead flowers are to child training. We can do the right thing for a long time, but if we let up and fail to diligently continue our training, that can have disastrous results. Little children illustrate this well. They need constant supervision at the beginning. As they grow older we find we can give them a little freedom. Their behavior lets us know what they can handle. If we give them too much freedom (forget to water the flowers), we can see poor results in their behavior very fast.

I thought my flowers were doing fine, and then all of a sudden they were dead. I had failed to notice they were starting to wither. If I had, I would have watered them, and they would have been fine. Our children's behavior does not deteriorate all at once. There are warning signs. Lack of respect, slow response to directions, and bad attitudes can develop slowly over time. When dealt with promptly, these problems are relatively easy to eradicate. But when left to grow, these problems can be significant. Even though it may seem that your children are thriving, make sure you pay attention to them. Watch for even the slightest withering of your training in their lives. You have made an investment in them; now watch your investment closely to be sure the yield is what you are looking for.

Do you watch your children closely enough to detect problems while they are small?

PRAYER

Heavenly Father, I need some help in this area. I find it difficult to stay current with so many children. I don't always see what they need. Help me to spend quality time with each child daily, so I can keep track of their needs better. My parenting skills must be better than my gardening skills or I'm in trouble. ⌒

FOOD FOR THOUGHT

1. Do certain children in your family need closer monitoring than others?
2. Invest the time when they are young for best results.
3. Ask God for the strength to follow up closely with all of your children. Meet their needs quickly. Small problems are easier to work with than bigger ones.

1 0 1

No Control

Then Job arose, and rent his mantle, and shaved his head,
and fell down upon the ground, and worshipped, and said,
Naked came I out of my mother's womb, and naked shall I return
thither: the LORD gave, and the LORD hath taken away;
blessed be the name of the LORD. In all this Job sinned not,
nor charged God foolishly.

JOB 1:20-22

As I drove alone in my car to the doctor's office, I felt numb. I was about to have my first ultrasound at six weeks of pregnancy. Having had my fifth miscarriage in eighteen months just a few months previous, I was anxious to see if we would see a heartbeat. Once again I had absolutely no control over what was going on in my life. Jim and I believe that God opens and closes the womb. We don't understand why I have had all of these miscarriages, but we believe as Job did: It is up to God.

The technician cautioned me that it might be too soon to see a heartbeat, but soon after she turned on the ultrasound machine, we saw a heartbeat. What a relief! I relaxed some after the good report and continued on with life. Last week I had a day where I was just sure the baby had died. I had experienced this type of thing before, and in the past it was always true. My mind was beginning to play games with me.

The next day I felt pretty sick, and then I became confused by my symptoms. For the next few days everything seemed okay, but I wanted to see the next ultrasound. Even though I had no control over what was happening, I had a strong desire to *know* what was happening. Again I drove to the doctor's office alone. I had prepared myself for bad news. Once again as soon as the ultrasound machine was turned on, I saw a heartbeat. Now at eight weeks I could see the tiny shape of a baby in the sac. What a relief! The heart rate and growth of the baby were exactly as they should be.

My baby is due when this devotional is scheduled to be released. God knew I would be trying to finish this book while experiencing the agony of the unknown in a new pregnancy. What a perspective He has given to me. It is out of my control. I can only respond appropriately as Job did when he suffered misfortune. He acknowledged that God gives and God takes away. I can understand that now. I don't know why it works this way, but I see that it does. Regardless of the outcome of this pregnancy, I know that we have honored God as we have understood His Word, and it is in *His* control.

Is there something in your life that you cannot control? God is the one in control.

PRAYER

Dear God, I give this baby back to You. If You wish for us to raise this child here on earth for You, we would love to do it. Your will, not mine. ❧

FOOD FOR THOUGHT

1. Do something special for someone you know who has had a miscarriage. She will appreciate your thoughtfulness.
2. Rejoice when you see God stretching your faith through trials.
3. Read the book of Job, paying close attention to his attitude. When you finish, ask yourself, what did I learn?

Editor's note: Jackie miscarried her baby at ten weeks gestation. Testing confirmed that there was a chromosome problem with the baby.

If this book has been a blessing to you and you wish to write me a note, or if you want to contact me for availability to speak at a conference, retreat, or seminar, I can be reached at:

EQUIPPING THE FAMILY
Attn: JMW
P.O. Box 458
Gridley, IL 61744-0458
(309) 747-4400

PERSONAL REFLECTIONS